HISTORY OF INDIAN MUSIC

HISTORY OF INDIAN MUSIC

With Particular Reference to Theory and Practice

By
BHAVANRAV A. PINGLE

LOW PRICE PUBLICATIONS
DELHI-110052

Distributed By:
D K Publishers Distributors P Ltd.
1, Ansari Road, Darya Ganj,
New Delhi-110002
Phones: 3278368, 3261465
Fax : 3264368
visit us at: www.dkpdindia.com
e-mail: dkpd@del3.vsnl.net.in

Reprinted in **LPP** 1999

ISBN 81-7536-178-6

Published By:
Low Price Publications
B-2, Vardhaman Palace,
Nimri Commercial Centre,
Ashok Vihar Phase-IV,
Delhi-110052
Phone: 7401672
visit us at: www.lppindia.com
e-mail: lpp@nde.vsnl.net.in

Printed At:
D K Fine Art Press P Ltd.
Delhi-110052

PRINTED IN INDIA

PREFACE

The present monograph neither pretends to be an exhaustive analysis nor aims at giving a complete description of Indian music or demonstration of the phenomena of Sound or of the elaborate history and laws of Music. Those who wish to study these subjects thoroughly, whether from their scientific or artistic aspect, must have recourse to special works and specialised studies.

To show briefly the broad outlines of Indian music as an art, and to test them by the light of Western science, has been the aim and seope of this discussion which, it is hoped, will be received with some interest by the public.

If there be anything acceptable to the general reader in this discussion, it is exclusively due to my drawing on the writings on the phenomena of Sound by Herbert Spencer, Charles Darwin and a few other English authors, which I have been studying for sometime. If there be anything interesting or instructive to the admirer of music, it is wholly due to the characteristics of Indian music itself which I have regularly studied for a long time.

The nomenclature used throughout this discussion, is not pure Sanskrit, but is the popular one among the Indian musicians, and, therefore, no strict rule of spelling is observed.

CONTENTS

CORRECTIONS

Page 37,	line 6	for	Zálás	*read*	Zhálás		
"	Do	" 13	"	through	"	though	
"	45,	" 24	"	Shodava	"	Shádava	
"	53,	" 17	"	carefnl	"	careful	
"	Do	" 40	"	alrs	"	airs	
"	115	" 35	"	th	"	$\frac{1}{4}$	

I.

THE HISTORY OF INDIAN MUSIC AND THE THEORY OF MUSIC IN GENERAL

It is an unwarrantable and speculative presumption to decide positively in the absence of reliable record, whether the singers of former times were much more accomplished than those of the present day, or *vice versa*.

In painting, carving, sculpture, architecture, and in the composition and execution of music, many persons would have us believe that we have, owing to our contact with Western civilizing influences, progressed. A judgment on the former arts can be formed by comparing the old things with the new ones, but a definite opinion on the merits and demerits of the by-gone singers, can only be substantiated by examining the music, its works, and its traditions which have come down to us from time immemorial. It is a fact beyond doubt, that the said music, its works, and traditions of Ancient Indian Aryas underwent alterations and modifications through many vicissitudes to which India has singularly been subjected.

Our judgment on the worth of Indian music is based on the ancient music, works, and traditions. The conclusion thus arrived at, might perhaps be flattering, or otherwise, because, we have no other alternative than to be guided by the aforesaid materials which have been handed down from generation to generation with certain additions and omissions. In such a state of things, it is very difficult to treat the subject with absolute impartiality, because it is a subject with which a considerable part of the Ancient Indian civilization is concerned. Suffice it to say, that the fact that music is a product of civilization, is as manifest as language or means of communication—spoken and silent, or written or otherwise expressed—is a means to education ; for though savages and rustics have their dance-chants and ceremonious vociferations, they are of a nature hardly to be dignified by the title musical.

The Indian musicians in spite of the absence of material encouragement in recent times, have preserved and protected the ancient plant of music from its total annihilation, and havegiven us an ancient legacy, which, though half dead, if properly understood, will considerably assist us to come to a right conclusion.

It is a well-known fact that the art of writing, though known for centuries to Indians, was hardly resorted to as a means to perpetuate their learning. The mode of transmitting knowledge or theory of things was in verses which were committed to memory by personal tuition, or as is said by Sir H. Mayne and others—Indian Aryas expressed their learning in a form of language so concise, as to fasten it on the memory, and finally to the fountain-head of their literature, which is admitted to be the oldest literature of Aryan race. The faculty of recollection (Indians are celebrated for their retentive memory) and the brevity of poetry for which poems are known, were so much developed, as to meet their want for accumlation of science, as an extension of the preception by means of reasoning or organized experience.

Language like an organized being, struggles for life, the better, the shorter, the easier forms gaining the upper hand.

Our by-gone writings are greatly mixed with foreign and imported matters, which have no relevancy whatever with music, but they were brought in, as necessary auxiliaries to it, when the art of music was thought to be a gift from the divinity of Anthropomorphites. In such a deplorable state of our writings, we are forced to depend more on inferences and deductions, than on direct evidence.

Indian traditions abound in instances such as

Haradása, Rámadása, Suradása, Tánasena, Lád, Kapola and their predecessors and successors too many to mention here. These artists in their respective times had made music their life-long study, and had been so much absorbed in it that most of them preferred to lead an ascetic life to worldly enjoyments, and thus became not only men of reverence and genius of their generation, but are even remembered and respected to this day on account of their keenness of sense in composition.

An unusually emotional nature is the general characteristic of musical composers. Stronger feeling produces stronger manifestation, and any cause of excitement will call forth from such a nature, tones and changes of voice more marked than those called forth from an ordinary nature. All music is originally vocal. All sounds are produced by the agency of certain muscles. These muscles in common with those of the body at large, are excited to contraction by pleasurable and painful feelings, and therefore it is, that feelings demonstrate themselves in sounds as well as in movements. Different qualities of voice accompany different mental states, and under states of excitement, the tones are more sonorous than usual. The sounds of common conversation have but little resonance, those of strong feeling have much more.

When we unbiasedly sift the roots of many sources of music, such as religious devotion and ceremonies, social performances, desultory works, and many a family of musicians in which it has so extensively been spread—and when we bring it in a systematized form to tell its own tale—we can safely affirm without fear of exaggeration, that it had once reached a higher stage of development than it is generally credited with.

The above assertion will be looked down upon by many as absurd, and even it will be thought paradoxical by right-thinking men, who justly admit that the Western education has successfully instilled and widely spread a new force of European growth into Indian thoughts and things, which have progressed and are still progressing, under the British supremacy, in refinements, arts, sciences, and in general knowledge.

The validity of the said assertion, however, is not an ideal one, but is based on reliable and reasonable sources, which form the subject-matter of this discussion. It is true, that we have no direct evidence of history in its narrow sense, but this difficulty can be overcome by critically examining the extant and traditional resources which go to form a history.

History, as is said, in its earlier stages, was regarded chiefly as a form of poetry, recording the more fabulous and dramatic actions of Kings, Queens, Heroines, Sages, Poets, Singers &c., and was sung as ballads by bards, and was told as legends or stories by story-tellers. History, as comprehended now, teaches us that the historical or great men were the histories or products of their societies. Without certain antecedents and a certain average national character, they could neither have been generated nor could have had the culture which formed them. If their societies were reinfluenced by them to a certain extent, they were both, before and after birth, influenced by their societies. They were the results of all those influences which fostered the ancestral character they inherited, and the social institutions they imbibed. So that such social changes which were directly attributable to individuals of unusual power, were still indirectly traceable to the social causes which produced these individuals.

Instead of enlarging on the elements of history, let us say that the justification of predicating the proposition—that Indian music was of higher origin and nobler development than it is generally voted to be and it is dying out for want of support—can be shown by reasonable inferences and deductions drawn from solid data. To do this we commence the discussion historically in its extended sense.

It is said of Tànasena, the famous singer of the latter part of the 16th century, that this wonderfully skiled and gifted artist sang so melodiously and so forcibly charmed the feelings of his hearers with his emotional cadences, that the kind and great Akbar, then Emperor, on hearing his performance styled him as a paragon of cadences. The vocalist was not only raised as one of the Emperor's immediate courtiers, an honour deservedly bestowed on those admitted to be specialists in their respective spheres of voçation, but was adulated as a personification of sound. It is a well-known fact that in our day instances never occur where similar infatuation, if infatuation meant appreciation and admiration, which played so effectively on Akbar, might take place. It is lamentable that we have got no immediate means to fathom how many pious, heroic and noble hearts must have been impressed by different emotions,—how many bright eyes must have been made brighter, and how many fair bosoms must have heaved on hearing the dulcet notes and religious pathos of Suradása, Bhikudása, Kabiradása and other celebrities of past ages. What known and unknown conquests those artists must have performed in their times and places? But our present public are more circumspect and are taught to keep their feelings more under command than to give way to hasty expressions of delight in public, and they cannot be blamed for so doing, otherwise the world would not perhaps be edified thereby. Therefore the mask worn by the public to screen their emotional expressions may be said to be a necessary evil with which we must remain content, and must bring ourselves to be looked upon, as more intellectual than emotional!

To be dead to anynatural expression of emotion is simply impossible from a naturalist's standpoint of view. If any being is devoid of natural expressions, it necessarily follows that it is dead to the impressions which act as stimulants, technically called *reflex action*.

The law of reflex action teaches us, that an impression on the end of an *afferent* (sensory) nerve is conveyed to some ganglionic centre, and is thence usually reflected along an *efferent* (motor) nerve to one or more muscles which it causes to contract; nervous excitation always tends to beget muscular motion; and when it rises to a certain intensity, it always does beget it. Those external actions through which we read the feelings of others, show us that under any considerable tension the nervous system in general, discharges itself on the muscular system in general, either with or without the guidance of the will. It is manifest that emotions and sensations tend to generate bodily movements which are forcible in proportion as the emotions or sensations are intense.

It is proved that equal stimulants produce unequal effects on differently constituted and circumstanced species of animal, man included with his different stages of civilisation or advancement to adaptation. It is moreover proved, that as knowledge progresses, the mode of impressions and expressions, metaphysically called objective and subjective, becomes more complex and economical than simple and violent, in obedience the law of the least resistance and greatest traction or the resultant of the two, but none the less impressive and expressive in its total effect.

The following paragraphs, though long and many, completely show how the superfluities or original necessities are cast away and the economical or better adapted ones are acquired and accumulated.

It is an open secret that the art of writing is of later origin than that of speaking. It is said that the arts of writing and printing have descended from picture-language. The most primitive form of permanently symbolizing a thing, was by depicting it on wall, that is by representing something like the thing to be imitated. In process of time, as the symbols grew habitual and extensive, the most necessary became fixed and thus economized, and passing through the hieroglyphic and ideographic stages, the symbols lost all apparent relations to the things signified, just as the verbal language did.

Verbal language, according to H. Spencer, "consists at the beginning of symbols which are alike to the things symbolized as it is practical to make them. The language of signs is a means of conveying ideas by mimicking the actions or peculiarities of the things referred to. Verbal language is also, at the beginning, a mode of suggesting objects or acts, by imitating the sounds which the objects make or with which the acts are accompanied. It needs but to watch the gesticulations with which savage accompanies his speech—to see a Bushman or a Kaffir dramatizing before an audience, his mode of catching game, or to note the extreme paucity of words in primitive vocabularies to infer—that at first attitudes, gestures, and sounds were all combined to produce as good a *likeness* as possible of the things, animals, persons or events described; and that as the sounds came to be understood by themselves, the gestures fell into disuse leaving traces, however, in the manners of the more excitable civilized races."

With regard to the origin and development of language Charles Darwin says—"After having read on the subject—I cannot doubt that language owes its origin to the imitation and modification of various natural sounds, the voices of other animals, and man's own instinctive cries, aided by signs and gestures. When we treat of sexual selection, we shall see that primeval man, or rather some early progenitor of man, probably first used his voice in producing true musical cadences that is, in singing as do some of the *Gibbon-apes* at the present day; and we may conclude from a widely spread analogy, that this power would have especially created during the courtship of the sexes and would have expressed various emotions, such as love, jealousy, triumph, and would have served as a challenge to rivals. It is, therefore, probable that the imitation of musical cries by articulate sounds may have given rise to words expressive of various complex emotions. The strong tendency in our nearest allies, the monkeys, in microcephalous idiots, and in the barbarous races of mankind, to imitate whatever they hear, deserves notice as bearing on the subject of imitation. Since monkeys certainly understand much that is said to them by man, and, when wild, utter signal cries of danger to their fellows; and since fowls give distinct warning for danger on the ground, or in the sky, from hawks, may not some unusully wise ape-like animal have imitated the growl of a beast of prey, and thus told his fellow monkeys the nature of the expected danger? This must have been a first step in the formation of a language. As the voice was used more and more, the vocal organs would have been strengthened and perfected through the principle of the inherited effects of use—and this would have reacted on the power of speech. But the relation between the continued use of language and the development of the brain, has no doubt been far more important. The mental powers in some early progenitor of man must have been more highly developed than in any existing ape, before even the most imperfect form of speech could have come into use, but we may confidently believe that the continued use and advancement of this power would have reacted on the mind itself, by enabling and encouraging it to carry on long trains of thought which no more can be carried without the aid of words, whether spoken or silent, than a long calculation without the use of figures or algebra. It appears, also, that even an ordinary train of thought almost requires, or is greatly facilitated by, some form of language. A long succession of vivid and connected ideas may pass through the mind, without the aid of any form of language, as we may infer from the movements of dogs during their dreams. We have also seen that animals are able to reason to a certain extent, manifestly without the aid of language. The intimate connection between the brain, as it is developed in us, and the faculty of speech, is well shewn by those various cases of brain diseases in which speech is especially affected. There is no more improbability in the continued use of the mental and vocal organs leading to inherited changes in their structures and functions, than in the case of hand-writing, which depends partly on the form of the hand and partly on the disposition of the mind, and hand-writing is certainly inherited."

"Several writers have lately insisted that the use of language implies the power of forming general concepts, and that as no animals are supposed to possess this power an impassable barrier is formed between them and man. With respect to animals, I have already endeavoured to shew that they have that power, at least in a rude and incipient degree. As far as infants from ten to eleven months old are concerned, it seems to me incredible that they should be able to connect certain sounds with certain general ideas, unless such ideas were already formed in their minds. The same remarks may be extended to the more intelligent animals. A dog forms a general conception of cats or speech, and knows the corresponding words as well as a philosopher. And the capacity to understand is as good a proof of vocal intelligence, though in an inferior degree, as the capacity to speak."

"Why the organs now used for speech should have been originally perfected for this purpose rather than any other organs, it is not difficult to see. Ants have considerable powers of intercommunication by means of their antennæ. We might have used our fingers as efficient instruments, for a person with practice can report to a deaf man every word of a speech, rapidly delivered at a public meeting; but the loss of our hands, whlist thus employed, would have been a serious inconvenience. As all the higher mammals possess vocal organs, constructed on the same general plan as ours, and used as a means of communication, it was obviously probable that these same organs would still be further developed if the power of communication had to be improved; and this has been effected by the aid of adjoining and well adapted parts, namely the tongue and lips."

"The fact of the higher apes not using their vocal organs for speech, no doubt depends on their intelligence not having been sufficiently advanced. The possession by them of organs, which with long continued practice might have been used for speech, although not thus used, is paralleled by the case of many birds which possess organs fitted for singing, though they never sing. Thus the nightingale and crow have vocal organs similarly constituted, these being used by the former for diversified song, and by the latter only for croaking."

According to modern researches, the voice is a transformation or equivalent of the respiratory movements. The respiratory mechanism with its adjuncts, in addition to its respiratory function, becomes of service in the case of man, animals, birds, and some insects, as a means of expressing emotion. The respiratory column of air, moreover, in its exit from the chest, is frequently made use of, in a mechanical way to expel bodies from the upper passages. Hence arise a number of peculiarly modified and more or less complicated respiratory movements such as sighing, coughing, laughing &c, to secure special ends, which are not distinctly respiratory. But as we have to confine solely to vocal sound, we of necessity should not enlarge on the movements of the organ of respiration. The vocal organ is nothing more than a wind instrument :—A blast of air, driven by a more or less prolonged expiratory movement, throws into vibrations two elastic membranes, the *Chorde Vocales*. These impart their vibrations to the column of air above them, and so give rise to the sound we call voice.

The emission of sound by the organs of voice in many kinds of animals, man included, is efficient in the highest degree as a means of expressions. When the sensorium is strongly excited, the muscles of the body are generally thrown into violent action, and as a consequence loud sounds are uttered, however silent the animal generally may be.

The phenomenon of sound, which is most interesting and instructive to us, is produced by the organs of voice in man, under different sensations and emotions. The vocal sound, as an indispensable interpreter of our thoughts and feelings, and the peculiar sounds and noises of animals, which express their wants and emotions, pleasurable and painful, are caused by the reflex action.

Charles Darwin philosophically says :—"Through man's power of intellect, articulate language has been evolved, and on this his wonderful advancement mainly depended. A physiological analysis of the faculty of language shews, that even the smallest proficiency in it might require more brain power than the greatest proficiency in any other direction. This faculty has justly been considered as one of the chief distinctions between man and other lower animals. But man is not the only animal that can make use of language to express what is passing in his mind, and can understand more or less, what is expressed by another. A kind of money, when excited, utters at least six distinct sounds, which excite in others of its kind, similar emotions. The movements of the features and gestures of monkeys are understood by us, and they partly understand ours."

"It is a more remarkable fact that the dog, since being domesticated, has learnt to bark in at least four or five distinct tones. Although barking is a new art, no doubt the wild parent species of the dog expressed their feelings by cries of various kinds. With the domesticated dog, we have the bark of eagerness, as in the chase ; that of anger, as when growing ; the yelp or howl of despair, as when shut up ; the baying at night ; the bark of joy, as when starting on a walk with his master, and the very distinctive one of demand or supplication on wishing for a door or window to be opened, How the barking of the dog, which serves to express various emotions and desires, and which is so remarkable from having been acquired since the animal was domesticated, and from being inherited in different breeds, was first learnt, we do not know ; but may we not suspect that imitation has had something to do with its acquisition (to meet new conditions or environments) owing to dogs having long lived in strict association with loquacious an animal as man ?"

"The habitual use of articulate language is, however, peculiar to man, but he uses, in common with the lower animals, inarticulate cries to express his meaning aided by gestures and the movements of the face. This especially holds good with the more simple and vivid feelings, which are but little connected with higher intelligence. Our cries of pain, fear, surprise, anger together with their approximate actions, and the murmur of a mother to her beloved child, are more expressive than any words."

"That which distinguishes man from the lower animals, is not the understanding, for every one knows, dogs understand many words and sentences. It is not the mere articulation which is our distinguishing character, for parrots and other birds possess this power. Nor is it the mere capacity of connecting definite sounds with definite ideas, for it is certain that some parrots, which have been taught to speak, connect unerringly words with things, and persons with events."

"Language is an art. It differs, however, widely from all ordinary arts, for man has an instinctive tendency to brew or bake. Moreover no philologist supposes that any language has been *deliberately* invented. It has been evolved and unconsciously developed by many steps. The sounds uttered by birds offer, in several respects, the nearest analogy, for all the members of the same species utter the same instinctive cries expressive of their emotions ; and all the kinds which sing, exert their power instinctively ; but the actual song, and even call-notes are learnt from their parents or foster-parents. These sounds are no more innate than language is in man. The first attempt to sing may be compared to the imperfect endeavour in a child to babble. The young males continue practising for ten or eleven months. Their first essays show hardly a rudiment of the song. Nestlings which have learnt the song of a distinct species, as with the canary-birds educated in the Tyrol, teach and transmit their new song to their offsprings. The slight material differences of song in the same species inhabiting different districts may be appositely compared to provincial dialects; and the songs of allied, though distinct species may be compared with the languages of distinct races of man."

"The birds appear to be the most æsthetic of all animals, excepting of course man, and they have nearly the same tastes for the beautiful as we have. This is shewn by our enjoyment of the singing of birds."

The foregoing details by H. Spencer and Ch. Darwin show that an instinctive tendency to acquire an art is not peculiar to man; and that the lower animals differ from man solely in his almost infinitely larger power of associating together the most deversified sounds and ideas; and this obviously depends on the higher development of his mental power.

It is evident that mere words are dull sounds if they are not accompanied by different accents and force, and that the same sounds, if differently modulated, produce different ideas. These modifications of voice, produced by feelings in others can be engenderd. Add to this voice, expressions and gestures of face, which give life to the otherwise dead sounds in which the intellect utters its ideas and enable the hearers, not only to understand the state of mind they accompany, but to participate in it. All speech is composed nominally of two elements, but in reality they are so inseparably interwoven that we cannot draw a line, where the words end and the tones, in which they are uttered, begin. But we can say that the words are the signs of ideas and the tones are those of feelings. It is true that certain articulations express the thought, while certain vocal sounds convey more or less of pain or pleasure which the thought gives. Using the phrase "vocal expression" in an extended sense as covering all modifications of vocal sounds, we may say that vocal expression is a means for the conveyance of thoughts and feelings. This double function of even spoken language is dimly recognized, but in practice we invariably find that more weight is attached to the tones than to the words, and the former are more relied upon than the latter.

Professor Max Muller rightly says—"we may speak in singing, and sing in speaking ; we may speak in whispering and whisper in speaking, we may even sing in whispering, and whisper in singing ; in fact we seldom speak without either singing or whispering certain portions of our words."

The tones of speaking, of reciting, and of singing severally exemplify one general principle—that the tones of excited feelings are more sonorous than those of common conversation, because muscular action is directly proportional to mental excitement. Expressiveness of speaking, of reciting, and of singing, is a question of tones, for these three phases of vocal sounds, under which all vocal phenomena are explained, are interchangeable one into other by the admission or dismissal of the variety and duration of tones.

Music, which is said to be the most powerful of all arts, has been evolved from its most primitive function in a great number of animals, man included with his different stages of development—to charm and call the opposite sex ; and that in man's advanced state of civilization it has been evolved to emotionally express the most complex sentiments, which intellectual or articulate language and poetry could not express. To add more to the vocal charms, science began to invent many musical instruments or supplementary senses, which, in animals, are confined to bodily movements, intensely performed during the pairing season on the earth, in the water and in the air.

Dr. Samman most thoughtfully said :—"we can concentrate greater intensity of feeling in a single musical note than any pages of writing."

Our nature is such that feeling and intellect are the two sides of man or the two expressions of the same thing, because there could be no feeling without intellect and intellect without feeling. Every student of philosophy or *unification* of knowledge knows that no thought is possible without things thought of ; and in addition, we may treat intellect and feeling objectively, and infer that no thought or intellect is possible without emotion or feeling of pain or pleasure which is its attribute, and that complexity of thought or intellect involves complexity of emotion or feeling and that complexity of impressions involves complexity of expressions.

It is true that the highest intellectual manifestations imply a good balance of the highest feeling ; but it is also true that the highest intellect is possible only with the highest feeling. They are so inseparably interwoven that we can not draw a line of *demarcation* where intellect or thought begins, and emotion or feeling proper to that intellect or thought ends, or *vice versa*. The tissue of every thought or feeling resolves itself into affections of consciousness. What we call affections of consciousness are subjective states of objective forces.

Instead of treating the above subject at length, suffice it to say that if higher intellect is a product of civilization, so is also higher emotion of the same agency.

Apart from the above considerations, which belong more to natural sciences and philosophical speculations than to music proper, let us consider what was the state of Indian society in which those wonderful singers, of whom we have spoken before, had lived, and what is the present state in force. From all that can be gathered, it seems, that in former times there were a few fine voices in existence in each generation as is the case now. But in our day there appears to be an amount of affectation, which if dilated upon, would at once seal the fate of many who pass as artists of no mean calibre. Besides, are the present classes so capable of knowing music as they were in former times, and have we got the same opportunities and facilities to indulge in it ? Is it too much to say that music as an art is not at all understood except by a microscopic few, who are probably prejudiced in favour of an artist or two whom they delight to pet and flatter ? Are not our educated men quite indifferent to music, partly for its objectionable surroundings and partly for their want of taste for it ? Nobody cares for its revival and encouragement, because the present well-to-do persons are not generally alive to its charm, and those who like it and practise it, are hardly beyond their immediate wants to compete for the race of life owing to the changed circumstances. Lastly, what steps have been taken to solicit the State patronage towards learning music as such ? To suppose that music will be resuscitated and systematized without the necessary support from State, is too idle a dream to be realized. Owing to the present educational policy of Government and the report of the last Education Commission, no hope is held out of any movement in the direction of State help. Government are quite in the dark about the true value of Indian music. They paid neither attention nor rendered help to it which they did to Indian literature, prose and verse. Unless music forms a part of the curriculum of schools and colleges, as do the classical and vernacular languages and even athletics, and unless some enterprising European scholars of music devote themselves to its regeneration, there will be neither its revival, nor will it be brought to such a system as would meet the wants of modern society. The most elementary way to teach music is to make the pupils recite their poetries to Harmonium or such other instruments as an accompaniment, and thus to cultivate a taste in youths to produce voice musically, and to appreciate it. It is really most rude and rustic to hear poetry recited in our educational institutions without the least regard for concordance. Indians never did any progress independently of the ruling power. Men, who have closely studied the problems of Indian administration, say that the Indians are so unpatriotic as not to be able to do substantial things without assistance from State, because they have been subjected from time immemorial to a despotic Government—a Government in which every thing is done for the people and nothing by them.

It will not be out of place here to mention, that even the Muhammadans partonized Hindu music to the best of their means, notwithstanding the inclemency of their religion to music in any form. It is a fact that the Muhammadans took a liking for music when they were sufficiently tempered by converts, intermarriages, contact with Hindus, and by acclimatization, and when they looked upon India as their adopted home. It is true that the Muhammadans had spoilt and checked every progress of Hindu thoughts and things in the beginning of their conquests and consolidation of their power and authority. But eventually they not only adopted Hindu music as an ennobling art, resorted to it with certain alterations as an additional force to their Marshiàs and Sojas, which are composed and sung in the sacred memory of their Imáms, Hásen and Husen. It is exceedingly probable that the love with which Hindu music inspired the Muhammadans was considerably due to the intolerance of their religion for natural expressions of emotion. They had brought with them their arts and poetry for which they were celebrated, but no music. As a matter of course, their patronage and intercourse were so powerful and forcible that they changed the features of original music, and wonderfully separated it from its parent stock. This fact can be verified by comparing the Sanskrit music (which is very rare in its original purity) of the Southern India with the Hindustani one. Hindustani music is a mixture of the Aryan origin or development and Muhammadan cultivation, and Sanskrit music of the Southern India is a mixture of the Aryan origin or development and Dravidian cultivation. Be this as it may, we find these two principal schools of Indian music, which do not so materially differ from each other, as the Aryan and Dravidian families of languages do.

It is said, that the ancients must have heard an amount of sweet and plaintive voices, because no ceremony, either religious or social, was performed without music. Music was thought to be a necessary part not only of secular enjoyments and of religious devotion, but of boody warfares and funeral ceremonies. Music is said to have been performed by a number of devotees by day and by night. Temples and halls are said to have been thronged by numerous musicians and bards. It is said that music was so much developed and spread that different melodies were fixed for differnt parts of the day and night and even season melodies were invented. Every village of importance had a bard or minstrel of its own who entertained his village patrons by extolling the deeds and personalities of great men and women, or by singing poems of morality inculcated by great sages. Those sages were revered who were more stoic than epecurian. It is believed, that the art of music was the principal enjoyment of the ancient Aryas, because they had a limited number of arts and sciences to attend to.

It is said that there were many musicians in possession of lands free from State imposition. This method of patronizing music was of great antiquity. Rávan of Rámáyan, according to traditions, had given a large province to his musicians, and he was himself proficient in music. Almost all the kings, who governed Ancient Indians, were more or less patrons or artists of music, and they were given special instructions in it. Even Royal ladies were not prohibited from acquiring the arts of singing, dancing and gesticulation.

In short, looking at the historically fabulous number of musicians who were employed in religious, political, and social institutions, and looking at the method of their music, we are forced to admit that the ancients had a considerable taste for music. Arts like comodities are improved only by their corresponding demands. It is said that as a relic of former times, we have many religious and itinerant singers who are spread all over the country, and that they show in a wonderful degree the sweetness and plaintiveness of voices which are attributed to the hereditary transmission and development of them.

Many will be surprised when we say that music is not only a sign of gratified feelings but it is a means to acheive them, and hence the songs of begging are a force to create sympathy. It will, perhaps, be objected that the function of creating sympathy in others allotted to singing, is more reproachful than complimentary, but a thoughtful consideration will lead them to the opposite conclusion. The utilitarian principle or the *summum bonum* is the tendency of civilizations which replaces the individual gratification, by gratification resulting from, or involving the happiness of others.

It is true that the songsters of whom we have just spoken are generally minstrels who sing either to the Ektárá (one-stringed lyre), Morli (made of gourd), or to the Kinri (crude form of Sarangi or fiddle) heroic or religious narratives versified by themselves to music of their own composition, and thus unite the separate offices in advanced societies of poet, composer, and instrumentalist.

We have selected the above case as a typical one of the lowest form of music, to show that the progress from simple to complex was considerably displayed in the multiplied differentiations which each of them underwent in Aryan societies. Instead of dwelling here on the many kinds of dancing, poetry, and music, which must have in the course of Aryan civilization come into use, and instead of occupying space in dilating upon the progress of poetry, of the various forms of metre, of rhyme and of their general culture, let us confine our attention to the immediate subject in hand.

To recur to our subject, we say that we do not find a single class of Indians, however crude it may be in its social institutions, dead and depraved to music of its own. Some of the airs, which are sung by certain classes, are pleasant if musically performed. It was a common practice in former times to teach the youths their lessons in tones of music. This practice was considerably due to the oral transmission and verse literature. Every Hindu of high caste was taught more or less to praise and pray his divinity by certain intonations called. Vratta, Chhand, Prabandh, Gita &c. The Vrattas and Gitas, which have come down to us, are really pleasant if musically expressed, and they give us an idea of the poetical singing of ancient Hindoos. This class of singing has not at all been influenced by the Muhammadan intercourse on account of its religious bearing.

Those who have studied the above subject, pronounce that this class of singing has not been what we call singing, but nearly allied to it; and as such is much less remote from common speech than singing is. For poetical singing is in all respects, intermediate between speech and song. Its average effects are neither so loud nor so low as those of song. Its tones are less sonorous in *timbre* than those of song. Commonly it travels to a smaller extent from the middle notes, and it uses notes neither so high nor so low in pitch. Those intervals habitual to it are neither so wide nor so varied. Its rate of variation is not rapid. And at the same time its primary *rhythm* is less decided ; it has none of the secondary *rhythm*, which is one of the marked characteristics of song. And the last but not the least, its average duration of notes is neither so long nor so short as that of song.

Hindus were such devoted admirers of music that they worshipped it not only as an offshoot of one of the four sacred Vedas, but they composed their Sáma-Veda to be chanted or sung. Their Sutras and Shrutis were attributed to the music of Shiva, who was styled the king of kings of musicians according to Shivasutra Jálum. Ascetic or stoically abstemious Buddhists and Jains, too, were not indifferent to the charm of music. Even now, it is generally believed by Hindus that the royal way to win over the deity is to say its praise and prayer in music. Every religious act is performed either in singing, in bodily movements, or in muttering and in gesticulation. We cannot pass over without remarking that, even in the most advanced nations of the world, the praise and prayer are generally accompanied by music. This class of music, which is called devotional music, is used like an all-absorbing—engrossing and concentrating agency or force—to completely divest oneself of all the affairs of all-powerful and ever-felt secularism, and to impress on him or on her nothing but vague (though believed to be grand and solemn) influence of Him or Unknowable, and to render the possibility of knowing—! In the Chinese annals it is said, "music hath the power of making heavens descend upon earth." People who are religiously inclined, call music a divine art.

It will not be grudged to quote here Herbert Spencer's most thoughtful exposition of the vocal sounds. He says—"That the vocal phenomena have a physiological basis. They are so many manifestations of the general law that feeling is a stimulus to muscular action—a law confirmed throughout the whole economy, not of man only, but of every sensitive creature—a law therefore, which lies deep in the nature of animal organization. The expressiveness of those modifications of voice is therefore innate. Each of us, from babyhood upwards, has been spontaneously making them, when under the various sensations and emotions by which they are produced. Having been conscious of each feeling at the same time we heard ourselves make the consequent sound, we have acquired an established association of ideas between such sound and the feeling which caused it. When the like sound is made by another, we ascribe the like feeling to him ; and by a further consequence we not only ascribe to him that feeling but have a certain degree of it aroused in ourselves : for to become conscious of the feeling which another is experiencing is to have that feeling awakened in us, which is the same thing as experiencing the feeling. Thus these various modifications of voice become not only a language, through which we understand the emotions of others, but also the means of exciting our sympathy with such emotions."

Illustrious Charles Darwin says : "Music and impassioned speech become *intelligible* to a certain extent, if we may assume that musical tones and rhythm were used by our half-human ancestors during the course of courtship, when animals of all kinds are excited not only by the love, but by the strong passion of jealousy, rivalry, and triumph. From the deeply laid principle of inherited associations, music in this case would be likely to call forth vaguely and indefinitely the strong emotions of a long past age. We have every reason to suppose that articulate speech is one of the latest as it certainly is, one of the highest, of the arts acquired by man, and as the instinctive power of producing musical notes and rhythms is developed low down in the animal series, it would altogether be opposed to the principle of evolution, if we were to admit that man's musical capacity has been developed from the tones used in passioned speech. We can thus understand how it is that music, dancing, song and poetry are such ancient arts. We may go further than this, and believe that musical sound afforded one of the bases for the development of language. As the males of several quadrumanous animals have their vocal organs much more developed than in the females, and as a Gibbon, one of the anthropomorphous apes, pours forth a whole octave of musical sounds and may be said to sing, it appears probable that the progenitors of man, either the males or females or both sexes, before acquiring the power of expressing their mutual love in articulate language, endeavoured to charm each other with musical notes and rhythms. So little is known about the use of voice by quadrumana during the season of love, that we have no means of judging whether the habit of singing was first acquired by our male or female ancestors. Women are generally thought to possess sweeter voice than men and, as far as this serves as any guide, we may infer that they first acquired musical power in order to attract the other sex. But if so, this must have occurred long ago, before our ancestors had become sufficiently human to treat and value their women merely as useful slaves. The impassioned orator or bard, or musician, when he with his voiced tones and cadences excites the strongest emotions in his hearers, little suspects that it was the same means by which his half-human ancestors long ago aroused each other's ardent passions during their courtship and rivalry."

"Naturalists are much divided with respect to the object of the singing of birds. Montagu and a few others maintained that the males of song-birds and of many others do not in general search for the female, but on the contrary their business in the spring is to perch on some conspicuous spot, breathing out their full and amorous notes, which by instinct the female knows and repairs to the spot to choose her mate. Jenner Weir informed me that 'this is certainly the case with nightingale.' Beepsteen, who kept birds during life, asserts that 'the female canary always chooses the best singers, and that in a state of nature the female finch selects that male out of a hundred, whose notes please her most.' There can be no doubt that birds closely attend to each other's song. Weir had told me of the case of a bull-finch 'which had been taught to pipe a German Waltz and he was a good performer. When this bird was first introduced into a room where other birds were kept and when he began to sing, all the others consisting of about twenty linets and carriers, ranged themselves on the nearest side of their cages, and listened with the greatest attention to the new performer.' Many naturalists believe that the singing of birds is almost exclusively the effect of "rivalry" and "emulation," and not for the sake of charming their mates. This was the opinion of Daines Burrington and White of Selborne, who both especially attended to this subject. Burrington, however, admitted that 'superiority in song gives to birds an amazing ascendency over others,' as it is well-known to bird-catchers. It is certain that there is an intense degree of rivalry between the males in their singing. Bird-fanciers match their birds to see which will sing longest. I was told by Yarell that a first-rate bird sometimes sings till he drops down almost dead, or according to Beepsteen, quite dead from rupturing a vessel in the lungs. Whatever the case may be, male birds, as I hear from Weir, often die suddenly during the season of song. That the habit of singing is sometimes quite independent of love is clear, for a sterile hybrid canary-bird has been described as singing whilst viewing itself in a mirror, and then dashing at its own image; it likewise attacked with fury a female canary when put in the same cage."

The above facts, which are so philosophically and studiously expounded, show that we do like the sounds which habitually accompany agreeable and pleasurable feelings, and dislike those sounds which invariably accompany disagreeable and painful feelings. Music adopts all the sounds which we like and intensifies them more and more when it ascends to its higher and higher forms, and becomes music or language of emotion simply in virtue of thus intensifying them. Music is rationally supposed to have influenced man in making those involved cadences of common conversation by which he conveys his complex thoughts and feelings.

To return to the subject in hand we say that we have but a very small portion of the ancient music. A large quantity of classic music must ever remain sealed to us, because we neither possess the means to collect and decipher many manuscripts and music which are secreted in different quarters like a sacred and invaluable trust, nor we are conversant with the knowledge of old works and notations, nor we have any standard work and notation of the modern origin in force. These difficulties are partly due to the proverbial selfishness of Indian musicians who do not like to part with the secret of their art, and partly to the want of taste in the public at large. If we attempt to write on Indian music as a science, independently of European researches and resources, we have but very scanty means at our command to produce even a small treatise. Such a treatise can not stand the critical test of a devout student of music and convince an impartial judge that the modern treatment of it is as thoughtful as it was in the times when Shiva, Hanumán, Kanád, Nárad, Bharat, and Parijátak flourished. Kanád was right in saying that sound was propagated by undulations that sent wave after wave in all directions from a central point. Some of the maxims, which we find in some of these authors, are presented in an unorganized form, or they stand as isolated dogmas or empirical generalizations which are neither so clearly apprehended, nor so much respected, as they would be, were they reduced to some intelligible form.

When we unbiasedly look at the researches of Kanád and others we are forced to admit that the ancients had made a considerable progress in music, not only as an art, but as a science in the remotest period of their civilization. It is deplorable that the data, which must have been adópted by Kanád and others to propound their theory of sound, should permanently be lost and nothing left, except the simple generalizations of their researches, to show and prove specifically what were the means which had caused a theory of sound probable at such a remote time of antiquity.

Wilson said : "Music of Sanskrit composition must ever remain inadequately represented by any other tongue."

Max Muller says : "The orthography of Sanskrit is the most complete and the language inflectionable."

When Sanskrit language has been admitted on all hands to be one of the most inflective and grammatically finished languages of the civilized world, it seems inexplicable why its not only co-existent but the parent-stock—the language of emotion—is discarded and condemned as barbarous. It cannot be said to be a sane proposition that Indians were civilized only in expressing their intellect or though but they were barbarous in expressing their feeling or emotion. These two interwoven elements of voca expressions are the necessary result of civilized life.

Says Jones :—"Amongst Hindus of early age music appears to have attained a theoretical precision at a period, when even Greece was little removed from barbarism."

It is not too much it we postulate that the acheivement of the ancients must have been possible only inductively, and not otherwise, because, there is no deduction in the absence of induction. The two hav a common root and neither can go without the other.

We assert without fear of contradiction that th music and works on it, which have come down to us if properly fathomed to the bottom, abound in artistic scientific, and philosophical speculations. It is a fac that the works have scarcely been brought forward i a connected form, so we are obliged to collect the tenets more from a number of scattered fragment which are dispersed through works on mythology theology, and literature, than from a treatise exclusively devoted to the subject. When mythology and theology are duly eliminated, it seems simply absurd to deny that the ancients had made a considerable progress in music as an art as well as a science. Their inventions and researches of the musical scale, their treatment of the gamut, their distinction between sound and noise, their composition of so many Vratas, Gitas &c. and their selection of many Rágas and Tálas are too thoughtful to be trifled with.

It was not known only to Pythagoras and early geometers that the length of a free vibrating string influenced the pitch of the note it produced, but the ancient Aryas had discoverd a connection between the pitch and its number of vibrations.

Captain Day, in his notes on Indian music says: "As regards the apparent similarity of the Indian and European scales, it must be remembered that the later were evolved, in process of time, from those of Ancient Greece. * * * The historian Strabo shows that the Greek influence extended to India, and also that Greek musicians of a certain school attributed the greater part of the science of music to India."

We give in the next chapter a comparative ratio of European and Hindu theories of gamut, not with an object to refute the European theory, which is presumed to be correct, but to support the above facts.

It should be borne in mind that, however the ratios may theoretically differ between the European and Hindu theories of (Grám) gamut, practically that is not the case. That which is discordant to one is also to the other. The difference lies only in composing the notes which form a musical piece, but not in the notes themselves.

II

THE THEORY AND PRACTICE OF MUSICAL SOUNDS

The name of "gamut" (Gráma or Saptak) is given to a series of seven sounds which succeed each other, proceeding from the grave to the acute, or *vice versa*. These sounds are comprised between two extreme Notes having the following character, namely, the highest sound is produced by double the number of the vibrations of the lowest. The most acute Note being the eighth of the series, the two extreme Notes are the octave of each other : one being the lower octave, the other higher one. If we now start from eighth Note, considered as the starting-point of a series of Notes similar to the first, and if we take care to strike a new series of Notes having between them the same degree of pitch as the first, it will be noticed that the impression left on the ear by their sucession, has the greatest analogy with that which results from hearing the Notes of the first scale. A melody, thus formed of a succession of Notes taken from the first series, preserves the same character if it is sung or played with the help of Notes of the same order taken in the second series. It would be the same if we formed in a similar manner one or more Gamuts, higher or lower.

A musical scale of the above kind formed of consecutive Gamuts, is unlimited, or at least has no other limits than those of our power of perceiving sounds.

We may remark that the Note from which we start to form a gamut is arbitrary. (In Europe for practical purpose they have conventionally adopted a fixed point of departure), because there is a vast number of similar musical scales placed by nature at the disposal of musicians.

In Europe the seven sounds are called C, D, E, F, G, A, and B. These letters are repeated for each octave. The same sounds are also called by other names, which are derived from the first syllable of each line of a Latin hymn, attributed to Paulus Diaconus.

The European and Hindu theories of Gamut (Saptak), if explained mathematically, stand thus :—

	1	2	3	4	5	6	7	8
European—	Do.	Ri.	Mi.	Fá.	Sol.	Lá.	Si.	Do.
	24	27	30	32	36	40	45	48
	1	2	3	4	5	6	7	8
Hindu	Sá.	Ri.	Gá.	Má.	Pá.	Dhá.	Ni.	Sá.
	22	26	29	31	35	39	42	44

Before going further, we give below the names of the 22 Shrutis (literally heard or perceived) as we find them in old works. The names are tolerably thus :—

(1) Tivrá, (2) Kamudvati, (3) Mandá, (4) Chhandovati, (5) Dayávti, (6) Ranjani, (7) Ratiká, (8) Roudri, (9) Krodhi, (10) Bajriká, (11) Prasárani, (12) Priti, Marjni, (14) Kshiti, (15) Raktá, (16) Sandipini, (17) Alápini, (18) Mandati, (19) Rohini, (20) Rammyá, (21) Ugrá and (22) Kshobhini.

Whatever Note we might conventionally select as a true Sá. (C) having a certain number of vibrations, the relation of all other Notes to it could be expressed mathematically, and this is done in the above theories.

The ratio of one sound to another is the determining cause of consonance and dissonance, or in other words, a musical scale is the melodious relationship of the number of vibrations (per second) of the Notes of which it (musical scale) is formed.

Sá. Ri. Gá, Má. Pá. Dhá. and Ni. are the initial letters of the names by which the seven sounds of Saptak (Gamut) are called, these letters are repeated for each octave. The names of the Notes seem to be as arbitrary as they are in Europe, though attempts have been made by early Hindus to justify them. The names are thus :—1st. Khashṭaja or Kharaja or Shaḍaja, 2nd. Rikhaba, 3rd, Gándhára, 4th. Madhyama, 5th. Paṇchama, 6th. Dhaivat and 7th. Nikháda.

Practically speaking, all the sounds (which are given in the above theories), in spite of their respective differences in the ratio of the number of vibrations per second which correspond to each of them, are classed—Shudh-Svaras (tones) and Komal-Svaras (half-tones or semi-tones). The Saptak (Diatonic scale) consists of seven Notes out of which five are tones—2nd Ri. 3rd. Ga. 5th Pa. 6th Dha. and 7th Ni.—and two are semi-tones 4th Ma. and the 8th or the first Sá. Excepting the 4th and the 8th or the first, which are already Komal (flat) or semi-tones, we can reduce or flatten the remaining five tones to ten semi-tones, and thus get in all twelve Notes (Chromatic Scale).

The above classification is in complete correspondence with the same that is adopted in Europe. But the peculiarity of the Indians is that though the Panchama (Sol. or G), when reduced to a half-tone, ought to be named Komal-Panchama (G Fl.), they in its stead call it Tivra or Kaḍi-Madhyama (F Sh.). All the semi-tones, excepting the two in the Diatonic scale—Sá and Má., are recognized by the name of Komal prefixed to the five tones of the Diatonic scale ; and why this half-Panchama (G Fl.) is excluded from the general rule, we do not know. Besides, no reasonable cause is shown in old works for this departure. It seems to be more conventional than logical to call a semi-tone once sharp (Tivra) and once flat (Komal), for we do not raise E (Gá.) and B (Ni.) to E sharp and B sharp, nor do we reduce F (Má.) and C (Sá.) to F flat and C flat

The names of the 12 Notes are these :—

(1) Shaḍja (C), (2) Komal-Rikhab (C Sh.), (3)

Rikhab (D), (4) Komal-Gandhára (D Sh.), (5) Gandhára (E), (6) Madhyam (F), (7) Tivra-Madhyam (F Sh.), (8) Pancham (G), (9) Komal-Dhaivat (G Sh.), (10) Dhaivat (A), (11) Komal-Nikhád (A Sa.) (12) Nikhád (B), and (13) Shaḍja (C, repetition of the first in the second octave).

The so-called sixteen and twenty-seven Shrutis, which are borrowed from some old works with much noise, are more fabulous than thoughtful, and the less we discuss them, the better. They run thus :—

Sá.	Ri.	Ga.	Ma.	Pa.	Dha.	Ni.
1	3	3	2	1	3	3—16
1	5	5	5	1	5	5—27

Physiologically, the range of an ordinary appreciation of tones lies between 40 and 4,000 vibrations a second *i. e.* between the lowest bass (C 33 vibrations) and the highest treble (C^5 4,224 vibrations of the Piano) : tones above and below these, even when audible, being distinguished from each other with great difficulty.

According to Indian idea of music, the limit of a voice (generally matured male) is three Saptaks (scales), one below (Anudátta), the register (Svaritta) and one above (Udátta) it. This is the general arrangement of their instruments. Indians were not satisfied with the 12 Notes (Chromatic scale), but increased the number of Notes under the names of Murchhaná (literally swoon, musically ¼th part of a tone) The number of Murchhanás is 21, but it ought to be 12 only. These Murchhanás are distributed over all the Rágas with the greatest advantage. The Indian scale with the aforesaid addition stands thus—5 tones, 2 semi-tones, or 12 Notes and 12 Murchhanás. We shall speak of the latter shortly.

Indian music is divided into two branches, *i. e.* Rágas (literally Ranj to please) and Ráginis or Bháryás (literally females). The characteristic distinction between a Rága and Rágini (diminutive of Rága), is that the former has in additions to tones and semitones, which are the only constituents of the latter, the principles of A'rohan (ascent or going from the grave to the acute), of A'vrohan (descent or going from the acute to the grave), of Murchhaná ($\frac{1}{4}$th part of a tone), of Gamak or Ghrashṭaka (literally that which slips, musically a connection of two or more Notes), of Meenḍ or Minḍ (literally resonant, musically a joining of two or more Notes on certain musical instruments), and of the total absence of accidentals.

Gamak or Ghrashṭak—or Meenḍ (now called Minḍ) is a way of sliding from a Note to other or others at a stretch ; it is not jumping, but it is an exceedingly attractive form of connecting two or more Notes. Minḍ or Ghrashṭaka is an impossibility on the Organ, Piano, Harmonium, Concertina and such other instruments, as long as they stand in the condition in which we find them. With due admiration for the real worth of European instruments, we are reluctantly constrained to say that, however slow or fast we may be in traversing from a Note to a Note on these instruments, the impression left on the ear is always of jumping, and not that of connecting two Notes. To give an idea of Minḍ or Ghasiṭ, corruption of Ghrashṭak, we give below a way to show how it is produced.

(1st)—SIMPLE JUMPING OF DIATONIC SCALE :—

1	2	3	4	5	6	7	8
Sá.	Ri.	Gá.	Má.	Pá.	Dhá.	Ni.	Sá.

(2nd)—SIMPLE JUMPING OF CHROMATIC SCALE :—

1	2	3	4	5	6	7	8
Sá.	K.-Ri.	Ri.	K.-Gá.	Gá.	Má.	T.-Má.	Pá.
9	10	11	12	13			
K.-Dhá.	Dhá.	K.-Ni.	Ni.	Sá.			

(3rd)—TRAVERSING BY MIND. DIATONIC SCALE :—

I 2 3 4 5 6 7 8

Sá. —Ri.—Gá.——Má.—Pa'.—Dha'.——Ni.—Sa'.

(4th)—TRAVERSING BY MEED : CHROMATIC SCALE :—

1	2	3	4	5	6	7
Sá.—	—K.-Ri.—	—Ri.—	K.-Gá.—	Gá.—	Má.—	T.-Má.—

8	9	10	11	12	13
Pá.—	K.-Dhá.—	—Dhá.—	K.-Ni.—	—Ni.-	Sá.

It is not fixed to produce a Meeḍ or Ghasiṭ of a particular Note from a particular Note, but the production depends on the capability of voice and instruments, and on the construction of Rágas. We shall speak of this subject in its proper course. It is not necessary to say that Meeḍ or Ghasiṭ may be an ascent as well as a descent. The line in the third and the fourth diagrams, which connects one Note to other or others, is the Meeḍ or Ghasiṭ. Many persons believe that in traversing by a Meeḍ or a Ghasiṭ from a Note to a Note or others, the intermediate Note or Notes must be touched, in spite of our desire, but practically that is not the case. Suppose, we ascend by a Meeḍ or Ghasiṭ from Sá (C) to Má (F), we can touch Má (F) from Sá (C) without producing the intermediate Notes —K-Ri. (C-Sh.), Ri. (D), K.-Gá. (D-Sh.) and Gá. (E). The same remark is applicable to a Meeḍ or a Ghasiṭ in descent. This fact can easily be verified on the fretted string instruments, such as Biná, Satára, &c.

Ghasiṭ is a peculiar way of sliding from a point to a point or points on the unfretted string instruments. It is a substitute for Meeḍ, and we shall speak of it presently.

Meeḍ and Ghasiṭ have been so much attended to by the Indian artists that they have constructed special instruments for them, such as Biná (Rudra Biná in Madras, Jantra, a primitive form, in Gujrat), Rabába, Sur-singár (not extant), Saroda, Satára, Sárangi (Indian fiddle), etc. The word Meeḍ, corruption of *Mand* (soft or dim), shows why it is not intended for a large audience, notwithstanding its charming effect. Credulous people fancy that the Biná is played by ten fingers, but only six fingers are used—3 of the right hand and 3 of the left hand. The usual musical limit of touching the Notes from a fret of the Biná or Satára by a Meeḍ, is five Notes, for instance from Sá (C) to Pá. (G). This limit is considerably changed when the artist moves from steal-wire to brazen-wire: this is due to the relative differences of densities, dimensions, and tensions of the respective metals. In Rabába, Saroda, Sárangi and such other instruments, or in the instruments having no frets, the limit of a Ghasiṭ is not fixed, because it can be produced by slipping over the wire from a point to any point, and not by stretching or drawing aside the wire at a point, which is done in the case of a Meeḍ. The characteristic distinction between a Meeḍ and a Ghasiṭ, is that the former connects the Notes by the tension of a wire; while the latter joins the Notes by reducing the length of a wire. Many artists prefer Meeḍ to Ghasiṭ, but musically speaking, the question seems to be more of taste than that of any intrinsic value; besides, certain instruments are fit only for Meeḍ, and certain for Ghasiṭ. The instruments, which are used for Meeḍ are long, fretted, (excluding Táus) and not played by a bow, and those, which are used for Ghasiṭ, are short, unfretted, stringed (not always metalic) and generally played by a bow. It may be remarked in passing that the Ghasiṭ can be produced on Biná and Satára, despite their frets; but the impression left on the ear, is not the same like the one produced by the Meeḍ.

The male voice is more adapted to Meeḍ or Ghasiṭ than the female voice. This is due to the relative shortness of the female vocal cords. We are not in a position to say that Meeḍ and Ghasiṭ are produced by the voice, but we are sure that the Ghasit is produced by it.

Since we want to speak at some length on Meeḍ or Ghasiṭ, we may describe the vocal sound in a few words.

In the voice, as in other sounds, we distinguish (1) Loudness. This depends on the strength of the expiratory blast. (2) Pitch. This depends on the length and tension of the vocal cords. Their length may be regarded as constant, or varying only with age. It consequently determines the range only of the voice, and not the particular Note given out at any time. The shrill voice of the child is determined by the shortness of the cords in infancy, and the voices of a soprano, tenor, and baritone are all dependent on the respective lengths of their vocal cords. Their tension is, on the contrary, variable ; and the chief problem connected with the voice, refers to variations in the tension of the vocal cords. (3) Quality or *Timbre*. This depends on the number and character of the over-tones accompanying any fundamental Note sounded, and it is determined by a variety of circumstances, chief among which is the physical quality of the cords.

According to Max Muller, "the average length of the vocal cords in man is $18\frac{1}{2}$ m. m. when relaxed, $23\frac{1}{2}$ m. m. when stretched ; in woman, $12\frac{2}{3}$ m. m. when relaxed, $15\frac{2}{3}$ m. m. when stretched : thus giving a difference of about one-third between the two sexes, which accounts for the different pitch of male and female voice."

Music with Meeḍ requires more exertion than without it, and such music is also slow. The same may be said of Ghasiṭ. Excellence in Meeḍ or Ghasiṭ is measured by the number of Notes connected in a given time.

It is accordingly probable, that the Meeḍ or Ghasiṭ is developed to express energy, resolution and decision. The action of the vocal muscles, which produces the Meeḍ or Ghasiṭ, is analogous to the muscular action which produces the energetic, resolute, and decisive movements of the body indicating these states of mind. Meeḍ or Ghasiṭ is so impressive and touching that it is redundant to say, that emotions are equally, if not better, expressed by connecting one Note to other or others, as by simple jumping from a Note to other or others.

Indian music appears to have been formed in two branches—Aláp (resonant) or Joḍ (literally joint, musically something like prelude) and Dhrupad (literally settled or moderate, musically a poetry set to music in Rágas and in certain Tálas, but not in Ráginis). The difference between Joḍ and Dhrupad, is that the former is completely free from poetry, and it is less restricted by a Tála (time-measure); the latter is fully restricted by a Tála, and it has less Meeḍs or Ghasiṭs. Joḍ can be sung or played only in Bilambpad (slow-going or *largo*) and Madhya (middle-moderate or *adante*) but not in Palut or Drut (fast or *presto*); while Dhrupad can pass through these three stages. Joḍ cannot be sung or played very fast, because it is simply impracticable to connect Notes with a rapidity which Palut (fast) presupposes. For instance—

Meeḍ—	1	3	5	5	6	8	8	10	12
	Sá.—	Ri.—	Gá.,	Gá.-	Má.-	Pá.,	Pá.—	Dhá.—	Ni.
Jamping—	1	3	5	5	6	8	8	10	12
	Sá.	Ri.	Gá.,	Ga.	Má.	Pá.,	Pá.	Dhá.	Ni.

Joḍ music is a later or advanced form of Dhrupad, and Dhrupad is a later form of the original Pads or Bhajans (prayer or praise). The Toma or Noma, the first word of Jod, looks to be an alteration of the Sanskrit "Oma," the letters Ṭ, Ḍ, T, Th, D, N, R, L, &c., and their peculiar combinations in Joḍ, are either arbitrary, or they are borrowed from the vocabulary of drum. Joḍ music is really charming for its fulness in Meeḍ or Ghasiṭ, and for its Murchhanás, in spite of the absence of words and of the technicalities of Tála (time). But now-a-days this class of music is very rare, it is found to a limited extent in the instrumental music, such as Biná, Saroda, Satára, &c.

The string instruments, which are not handled by a bow, are played very fast without Meeḍ or Ghasiṭ by Javá (a triangle piece of bone or ivory used on Rabába and Sarod) and Mijráfa or Nakhi (a triangle ring of wire used on Biná and Sátar). The Javá and Nakhi require but a very short time to give a stroke out and into a tensed cord of the aforesaid instruments. This facility of giving the strokes swiftly, has been taken advantage of by the instrumentalists to compose their own tunes, called Zálás and Gats. The former are played with Joḍ in Madhya (moderate time) like its accompaniment or complement on the last wire of Biná (in this instrument the last finger of the left hand is also used to touch a Chikárá), Sarod, and Satára ; the latter are played in Rágas and Ra'ginis. The Gats are nicely formed through they have only four technicalities, *i.e.* Da' Ḍa', Diḍ, and Ḍid or Ḍada'. The stroke which is given in, is named Da', and the out one is called Ḍa'. When the in and out strokes are combined and produced at the same time which Da' or Ḍa' takes, the combination is called Diḍ ; and this process of giving the strokes in and out if reversed, goes by the name of Ḍid or Ḍada'. There are hundreds of Gats in Sarod and Sata'ra music which are really artistic on account of their Meeḍ, Ghasiṭ, Murchhana' and Murki—an advanced form of the trill.

Murki (a collective name of Giṭakaḍi, Jam-jama', Khaṭka' and Sa'sa or A'sa) is less valued and respected than Meeḍ and Ghasiṭ. Musically speaking, Murki is eqnally, if not more, attractive as Meeḍ and Ghasiṭ. The cause of this disparagement seems to be that it is of later formation, and the female voice is better adapted to it than the male voice. This is due to the relative shortness of the female vocal cords. The differeuce in adaptations to Meeḍ or Ghasiṭ and Murki by the male and the female voices respectively, is a subject which admits of a generalization :—*All things being equal, no longer and the thicker the sonorous body, the better the Meeḍ or Ghasiṭ.—All things being equal, the shorter and the thinner the sonorous body, the better the Murki.*

To render the above proposition more rigorous, we must define the intensity or loudness and the pitch of sound in the words of Acoustics. The intensity of sound is determined by the amplitude of the vibrations : the greater the disturbance of the air or other medium, the intenser the sound. The pitch of sound is ascertained by the wave-length of the vibrations : the shorter the wavelength, the larger the number of consecutive vibrations which fall upon the ear in a second—the higher the pitch.

All things being equal, the longer the wave-length of the sonorous vibrations, the better the Meeḍ or Ghasiṭ—All things being equal, the shorter the wave-length of the sonorous vidrations, the better the Murki.

The above proposition can easily be verifled by changing the length and thickness of the wire of a string instrument. Even the change of thickness will give us an idea of it. It is probable that Murki is expressive of gentler and less active feelings, and that is so because, it implies the smaller muscular vivacity, due to a lower mental energy. Murki has wonderfully progressed in recent times owing to a special branch of music called Ṭappá (literally stage). They have considerably lessened the rigidity of Tála in order to encourage Murki. Music with Murki is slower than with Meeḍ or Ghasiṭ. Excellence in Murki is measured by the rapidity of strokes on two or three Notes in a given time. When this motion is moderate it is called Gitakaḍi or Jam-jamá, and when it is the lowest it is called Khaṭká or Sás or A'sa.

The distinction between Ṭappá and Khyál (literally attention, musically a later form of Dhrupad), is that in the former there are more Murkis than Meeds or Ghasiṭs, and it generally consists of Rágnis ; while the latter is always sung in Rágas, and it has more Ghasiṭs or Meeḍs than Murkis. The above distinction is not strictly observed now-a-days, for any kind of Chija (poetry set to music) is sung in Rágas as well as in Ráginis.

There is a class of singing which goes by the

name of Tirvaṭ-Tarắná and Chatarang. The former is formed only of the drum technicalities, or is a form of long-past poetry; the latter is a combination of poetry and the drum technicalities. This kind of singing is performed very swiftly, and Tála (time measures) seems to be the principal item to it, though it is sung in Rágas as well as in Ráginis.

The singing of Sargams (the initial letters of the Notes to be touched are set to music in Rágas and Ra'ginis—this way of singing seems to be ancient) is more accurate in Karnatic music than in Hindustani one, so far as the names of the Notes sung are concerned, but so far as the composition of Notes goes, Karnatic music cannot be said with impartiality to be superior to Hindustani.

Pada or Bhajan (oldest form of praise and prayer, or love-song of Krishna) Ṭhumri (love-song), Gazal, Rekta', &c. &c. are very common though musical. They are identical more with Nrtya (dancing) and Ha'va-Bha'va or A'rath (gesticulation) than with classical music. There are many songs of this description which are really lovely for their poetry and music.

The shaking of the body is one of the necessary results of certain passions, or perhaps all passions when pushed to an extreme. It is superfluous to remind ourselves that we have the trembling of anger, of fear, of hope, of joy; and that the vocal muscles being implicated with the rest of the body, the voice too becomes tremulous. This trembling (*Kamp*) of voice is not only taken advantage of by the Indian musicians, but its opposite—the principle of steadiness (Sthirata' or Thairna')—is marvellously observed by them.

The Principle of Ta'na (literally stretching or extending musically variation) is the common property of Khya'l, Ṭappa', Ṭhumri, Pada, &c. &c.

Ta'na or variability of pitch (simple jumping) is a characteristie of emotional speech. Instead of discussing this subject with its metaphysics, we must be content with the knowledge that the muscular excitement is shown not only in the strength of contraction, but also in the rapidity with which different muscular adjustments succeed each other.

The principle of A′rohan (ascent) and A′vrohan (descent) is so strict that even a slight change alters the Ra′ga into other Ra′ga or Ra′gini, as the case may be. Instead of treating this principle at length, suffice it to say that while speech is comparatively monotonous, singing makes use of wider intervals. Speaking voice seldom wanders over more than three (in some cases four) notes, above or below its medium, and that too by small steps, but the singing voice not only wanders over higher and lower Notes of its register, but goes from one Note to others by larger intervals.

Before going further, we must not omit to say that those which ordinarily go by the names of Rágin is are, practically speaking, Rágas. They are called Ráginis simply because their names end in "*I*," or possibly they may have been composed by women, or probably they may have been formed by men and sung in praise or love of women, as some names of the Ra′ginis suggest, such as Goudi or Gouri, Renki, Dhánashri or Dhànyastri, Shri or Stri, Lalita′, Ma′lashri &c. The real Ráginis—diminutive of Ra′gas—are known by the name of Dhun or Jilhá. The characteristic distinction between a Rág or Rágini and a Dhun or Jilhá, is that the former has a fixed number of Notes, no accidentals, a regulated arrangement of traversing the Notes upwards and downwards, and above all a number of Murchhanás ($\frac{1}{4}$ part of a tone); while the latter is free from so many restrictions.

The Murchhanás ($\frac{1}{4}$ part of a tone) are so charmingly distributed over different Ra′gas, that if taken away from them they (Ra′gas) considerably lose their effect. Murchhaná is always touched by Meed or Ghasit, but not otherwise. Those who have practised Indian Ra′gas, can easily understand why Darbári-

Kanaḍa is reduced to Sind-Bhairvi (a Jilhá) by eliminating only the Murchhanás. A mere taking away of the Murchhanás changes Sáhána:Kánáḍá into Káfi (a Jilhá), Jogia into Bhairvi (a Jilhá), Bágeshri-Kánáḍá into Báhár (a Jilhá) &c.

It is really a very difficult, if not an impossible, task to deal with the above facts without entering deeply into the primary and secondary composition of Rágas. The scope of this discussion does not allow us to do so, which would turn it into a treatise on Indian music. However, without unnecessarily swelling the body of this discussion, we shall briefly treat this subject in its proper place.

It is an open secret to those who have practised music (as an art), that the second stage of their progressive and successful study in the Saptak (Gamut), is the acquisition of a wonderful power to perceive the least difference between the unision (first acquirement) and the 8th Note of the Chromatic scale, or between Sá. (C) and Pa. (G). The third stage is generally Ga. (E). Broadly speaking, the unison and its octave are not separate Notes, but the latter reinforces some of the harmonics of the former. The wonderful sympathy of Sá. (C) with Gá. (E) and Pá. (G), which is called in Acoustics simple ratio or Harmony, is not only known to Physicists, but it is experienced by keen musicians to a great advantage as a test of the accuracy of a musical scale.

In place of the tuning-forks, which are used in Europe to adjust a musical scale, Indians use their acquisition of the perception of relation or sympathy of Sá. (C) with Ga (E) and Pá. (G) in the following simple but certain method to attune a musical scale with the greatest possible precision. First they adjust Sá. (C), Gá. (E), and Pá, (G), or A B C of Indian music (the perfect major chord), and then the remaining four notes—Ri. (D), Má (F), Dha'. (A), and Ni. (B) are tested thus :—Ri. (D) is tested with Dha. (A), Ma'. (F) with Sá. (C), and Gá. (E) with Ni. (B).

The sympathy between Ri. (D) and Dha. (A), Ma.

(F) and Sá. (C), Gá. (E) and Ni. (B), artistically speaking, is the same which exists between Sá. (C) and Pá. (G).

The above method teaches us that the 12 Notes (Chromatic scale) stand in sympathy with each other in the following way :—

	1		8	1		5
1	Sá. (C)	with	Pá. (G)	Sá. (C)	with	Gá. (E)
2	K. Ri.	„	K. Dha	K.-Ri.	„	Má.
3	Ri.	„	Dhá.	Ri.	„	T.-Má.
4	K.-Gá.	„	K.-Ni.	K.-Gá.	„	Pá.
5	Gá.	„	Ni.	Gá.	„	K.-Dhá.
6	Má.	„	Sá.	Má.	„	Dhá.
7	T.-Má.	„	K.-Ri.	T.-Má.	„	K.-Ni.
8	Pá.	„	Ri.	Pá.	„	Ni.
9	K.-Dhá.	„	K.-Ga′.	K.-Dhá.	„	Sá.
10	Dhá.	„	Ga′.	Dhá.	„	K.-Ri.
11	K.-Ni.	„	Ma.	K.-Ni.	„	Ri.
12	Ni.	„	T. Ma.	Ni.	„	K.-Gá.
13	Sá. (C)	„	Pa. (G)	Sá. (C)	„	Gá. (E)

The above method is called, in practical music, Sur-Bevrá or Bevdá,—this word (literally signifying double) is not an appropriate term.

The above description is a practical illustration of the *nodes* and *ventral segments* of the science of Acoustics, or of the perfect major chord, as it is called by some scientists.

We shall be wanting in doing justice to our immediate subjet in hand if we do not speak a word about the variety intensity and velocity of sound, and a word about noise.

The variety of sound depends on the forms and nature of the sonorous body, and on the way in which the sound is conveyed to our ears. The intensity of sound varies according to the density of the medium which propagates it. The velocity of sound is uniform at every portion of the distance traversed, and it is the same with sharp and dull sounds. Neither the line, nor the precision of a piece of music, is altered whatever may be its distance from the listener ; when the distance increases, all the sounds are lessened in the same degree.

Noise frequently proceeds from a confused mixture of different sounds, which the ear can scarcely distinguish from each other ; or in other words, noise is nothing but a sound the vibrations ot which do not last long enough to enable the hearer to appreciate the relative pitch.

Max Muller says :—"Noise is produced by irregular impulses imparted to the air, and tone is produced by regular periodical (issochronous) vibrations of elastic air."

According to N. Lockyer :—When two melodious sounds follow each other at a sufficiently short interval, the sensations are fused into one. When two sounds not quite in tune are struck together, the interference of the vibrations gives rise to an alternating rise and fall of the sound, known in Acoustics as " beats." When the beats follow each other, as rapidly as 132 in a second, they cease to be recognized, that is to say, the sensations which they cause, become fused. Before they disappear, they give a peculiar disagreeable roughness to the sound. The pleasure, which is given by musical sounds, depends largely on the absence of this incomplete fusion of the sensations

P Blaserna says :—" In the music of all nations two unfailing characters are found, rythmic movement and procedure by determinate intervals. The first appertains also to the speech and the other acts of man as walking, swimming, dancing, etc. ; the second belougs exclusively to music."

" All nations have selected notes to be used, have collected together those intended to be together, and have thus created one or more *musical scales.*"

" By musical scale is meant the collection of all the notes, comprised between the fundamental note and its octave. * * The studv of the musical scale gives one of the most important and concise means of judging of the musical state of a nation. * * * "

"It seems strange that a few notes put together in a musical scale should be able to acquire a true importance in the study of music. If it were a question of an assemblage of notes made at hazard or capriciously, the matter would be of no importance; but the musical scale is always the product of the musical activity of many centuries. It is not established before music, but is developed with it. A very perfect form of music must have a perfect scale; an imperfect and primitive form of music, on the other hand, will have a scale of little value."

"A musical sound is always a compound sound, its vibrations are more or less complicated, and it by itself constitutes a true harmony. * * It follows that in combining two, three, or more musical sounds in order to form a chord, it is not enough that the fundamental notes should bear simple ratios to each other, but it is also necessary that the harmonies should obey this law.".

A Bain says:—"Since a sweet note is already a harmony, the influence of the recognized musical concords is not something absolutely new, but an extension of the same harmonizing process. * * * The simple musical ratios ($\frac{2}{1}$ $\frac{3}{2}$ $\frac{4}{3}$ &c.) express the best chords, and, as the ratios are further removed from simplicity, the harmonious effect gives place to discord, which is at last painful."

We give in the next chapter an analysis of a few simple and compound Rágas.

III

THE RĀGAS AND THEIR FORMATIONS

The object of selecting the following Rágas for our discussion, is to show that there is but very little difference of opinion on their respective Sargams or skeletons. These Rágas, which are familiar to many, admit of being explained in the following tables without intricate technicalities. There are many finished compound Rágas, but they cannot be explained without exhaustive details, which do not form the subject-matter of this discussion. However, it should be borne in mind, that whatever conclusions we may arrive at after discussing the Rágas given below, they will hold good with all Rágas. which are practised, and not simply theorized.

It will not be out of place here to state, that there is a slight difference of opinion in the Sargams or skeletons of some of the Rágas which are practised by artistes of different schools. This difference is considerably due to the oral transmission af Rágas for many generations, although they were once committed in writing, and not orally taught, as they are done even at the present day.

All Rágas are divided into four divisions—1st Odava (consisting of 5 Notes), 2nd Kha'ḍava or Shoḍava (consisting of 6 Notes), 3rd Sanipurná (consisting of 7 Notes), and the 4th Sankirna (literally gleaned, consisting of seven or more Notes, and their arrangement of ascent and descent is not the same which is in the first three divisions, and, therefore, we call them Misra, or compound Rágas).

In order to understand the following three tables, let us refresh our memory by saying that the Saptak (Diatonic scale) consists of 5 tones and 2 semitones, or 12 Notes (Chromatic scale), the 13th is the repetition of the first in the second octave ; and that the

Indians call the 7th Note (which is a semitone, and ought to be named Komal-Komal-Pancham (G Fl.) Tivra or Kaḍi-Madhyam (F Sh.)

The arrangement, which is adopted in the following tables, is so simple that no lengthy explanation is needed. The Rágas are not arranged in an alphabetical order, but they are given under the four heads Oḍhava, Khaḍava, Sampurna, and Sankirna with the numbers and names of the Notes which they cover. In the first three classes, which are given in the first table, the order of ascent and descent is the same. In the fourth class (Sankirna), which is given in the second table, the order of descent is different from that of ascent, and some of them contain more than 7 Notes. In the third table, the order of ascent and descent is not the same, and, therefore, they are separated from the Sankirna in the second table. Those who are acquainted with the first two tables, will find no material change in the third table, except Sá (C)—second which is introduced on the second line to indicate the orders of ascent and descent.

The initial letters, which are used in the following tables, and in the subsequent discussion, are these :—(1) S for Shaḍja, (2) K-R for Komal-Rikhab, (3)R for Rikhab, (4) K-G for Komal-Gándhár. (5) G for Gàndhár, (6) M for Madhyam, (7) T-M for Tivra Madhyam, (8) P for Pancham, (9) K-Dh for Komal-Dhaivat, (10) Dh for Dhaivat, (11) K-N for Komal Nikhád, (12) N for Nikhád, and (13) S for Shaḍ which is the repetition of the first in the second octave (Ashṭak).

Since we have concisely defined the artistic meaning of the word Rága in the last chapter, we need not interest ourselves, at this stage of our discussion, with its dialectics ; nor can we venture to trace its origin historically. The most that we can say concerning the word "Rága" (Ranj to please), is that it is intended, from time immemorial for certain combinations of the musical notes with certain elaborations, which we have already briefly stated.

We shall dilate on the subject a little, after studying the skeletons of the Rágas. It is neeessary to say that many of the Rágas, which are given in the table are too old, as their names imply.

However several the above Rágas may appear at first sight, in reality they show formations of certain combinations (chords) of Notes, which we class under the following eleven groups. The groups run thus :—

1st –Rágas with Komal-Rikhab (C Sh), followed by Komal-Gandhára (D Sh.) in ascent, and *vice versa* in descent, are—Jogia or Jilhá-Bhairvi, Gurjari, Toḍi and Mul-táni (K-R, not in ascent).

2nd—Rágas with Komal-Rikhab (C Sh.), followed by Gandhára (E) in ascent, and *vice versa* in descent are—Bibhása, Kámkali or Gunkali, Lalat, Lalita or Lalat, Jaita, Puriá or Renki, Márvá or Dipak, Soheni, Basant, Kálangḍá-Jilhá, Purvi. Dipak or Puriá-Kalyána, Paraja, and Purvi-Hindi.

3rd –Rágas with Komal-Rikhab (C Fl.), preceded by Gandhára (E) in descent, are—Jogiá, Shri, Bhairava or Jilhá-Kalangḍá, Jaitáshri, and Málava.

4th—Rágas with Rikhab (D), followed by Komal-Gandhára (D Sh.) in ascent, and *vice versa* in descent are –Nàyaki-Kánaḍa, Madhur-Kánaḍá, Darbári Kánaḍá or Jilhá Sind-Bhairvi, Sáhánà-Kánaḍá or Jilhá-Ka'fi, Dha'ni Ka'náḍa', Sind-Ka'náḍa' or Jilha'-Ka'fi, and Jejevanti-Kána'ḍ or Jilha'-Sindora'.

5th—Ra'gas with Rikáab (D), Preceded by Komal Gàndha'r (E Fl.) in descent, are—Gàndha'r or Jilhà Sind-Bhairvi, Miàki or Ta'nsen's Malha'r. Pala'sa or Jilhà-Sind-Bhiarvi or Jilha', Dhana'shri or Jilhà Kafi, Jounpuri, Ba'geshri Kànaḍa' or Jilhà-Ba'ha'r, and Bhim pala's or Jilha' Sind Bhairvi.

6th –Ra'gas with Rikhab (D), followed by Ga'ndha'ra (E) in ascent, and *vice versa* in descent, are—Bhupa or Bibha'sa, Bhupáli, Jangalà, Kalyána Bilával Alaiá Bilával Yaman Kalyàna Hàmir, and Nàṭa.

7th—Ra'gas with Rikhab (D), preceded by Ga'ndhára (E) in descent, are—Deshási, Soraṭa or

Jilhá Khamách, Desa, Gounḍ, Kámoḍa, Bhyágaḍá, Bhyága, Shankara' Bharan, Shankara', Keda'rà, Chha'ya', Gounḍ Malha'r, and Gouḍ Sa'rang (G or E is seldom touched in descent.)

8th—Ra'gas with Rikhab (D), followed by Madhyam (F) in ascent, and *vice versa* in descent, are—Megh or Sur-Malha'r, Brinda'bani-Sa'rang, Sur-Sarang, Baḍahans Sa'rang, Madhuma't Sa'rang, Ra'mada'shi Sa'rang, and Gouḍ-Sa'rang (the last is a misnomer, as it has but very little similarity with other Sa'rangs

9th—Ra'gas without Komal (flat) or Shudha (Diatonic) Rikhab (D), but with Komal Gandha'ra (D Sh.), fol lowed by Madhyam (F) in ascent, and *vice versa* in descent, are—Ma'lkosa and Koushi.

10th—Ra'gas without Komal (flat) or Shudha (Dia tonic) Rikhab (D), but with Gandha'ra (E) follow ed by Madhyam (F) in ascent, and *vice versa* in descent, are—Banga'li Tilanga or Banga'li, Khamba'ti, Deshi and Khamàcha.

11th—Ra'gas without Komal (flat) or Shudha (Diatonic) Rikhab (D), but with Gandha'ra (E), followed by Tivra-Madhyam (F Sh.) in ascent, and *vice versa* in descent, are—Màleshri Hinḍola, and Pancham.

The classification of all the Rágas into eleven groups, is not quite scientific, but it helps us to draw the following conclusions :—

1st—There is not a Rága, simple (Oḍhava, Khoḍava and Sampurna) or compound (Sankirna), which covers the 12 Notes (Chromatic scale).

2nd—There is not a Rága which has less than six Notes from the register or fundamental S (C) to the S (C) in the second octave.

3rd—There is no Rága which has two Rikhabs (Ds), Komal (flat) and Shudha (Diatonic), or two Dhaivats (As), Komal (flat) and Shudha (Diatonic).

4th—There is a Ra'ga which has two Ga'ndha'rs (Es), Komal (flat) and Shudha (Diatonic) –5th in the second table.

5th—There are Ra'gas which have two Panchams (Gs) or Tivra-Madhyam (F Sh. or G Fl.) and Pancham (G)—9th, 14th, 25th, 26th, 29th, 33rd, 34th, and 39th in the first table, 1st, 3rd, 13th, 17th, 19th, 21st, 23rd, 24th, and 25th in the second table, and 1st, 2nd, 6th, and 9th in the third table.

6th—There are Rágas which have two Nikháds (Bs), Komal (flat) and Shudh (Diatonic)—40th, 41st, and 42nd in the first table, 4th, 6th, 9th, 12th, and 25th in the second table, and 2nd and 3rd in the third table.

7th—Every Rága must have either G (E), M (F), or P (G); and that there is not a Rága which has Shudh-Rikhab (D) without Pancham (G); and that there is not a Rága which has Shudh-Rikhab (D) and Komal-Dhaivat (G Sh) without the intercession of Komal-Gandhára (E Fl).

Instead of giving a long dissertation on the composition of the above Rágas, we allow them to stand as they are. If we attempt to analyse each and every Rága, we are sure to exceed the limits of this discussion, and to launch into deep technicalities, which, from the beginning of our discussion, we have tried our best to avoid without compromising it.

It will be too far to presume to find out a reasonable cause to show why two Rikhabs (Ds), or two Dhaivats (As) were thought to be incongruous or incompatible for a Rága, when two Gandhárs (Es), two Panchams (Gs), and two Nikháds (Bs) were selected to be harmonious or artistic for a Rága. The omission of two Rikhabs (Ds), or of two Dhaivats (As) for a Rága, properly speaking, seems to be a question of mere accident or non-occurrence. However, it can positively be said that most of the Rágas, which are given in the above tables, are highly melodious. These Rágas show a wonderful degree of the thought and labour spent by the by-gone generations in combining the Notes to form so many Rágas without allowing them to be confounded one with the other. It cannot be denied that the said Rágas are quite distinct from each other, and that they are highiy finished. It cannot be said with fairness that so many Rágas were the formation of arithmetical calculus, but in reality, they were the necessary manifestation and results of the antiquated Aryan invention and Mahomedan cultivation of music, as an art.

It is opportune to say that instead of simply traversing along the Notes of a Rága in a given time from one octave to other or others, they begin their Rága first in Kharaja (one octave below the register), then they go to A'sthái, corruption of Sthái (the register octave), thence to Antará (one octave above the register), and finally they end it in S (C or tonic) of the first or register octave : thus covering three octaves, one below (Anudátt) and one above (Udátt) the register (Svaritt) octave.

The ordinary class of singing, which deals in Chija (poetry set to music), and with which we very often come in contact in ordinary performances, is not extended beyond the register (Svaritt) octave. The Chija-singing, as a class, contains more words than music, and the words are done away with in Tána (variatian), in Murki (an advanced form of the trill), and in Mind or Ghasit (not jumping). It is true that Chija-singing of some of the Rágas does not always begin from the register (Svaritt) S or tonic, for instance, in Hámir and Bhupa or Bibhás. These two Rágas generally begin from Dh (A).

To extend the variation of the Notes in a Rága, without breaking through the rigid principle of ascent and descent they go in this way, for instance, in Bhupa or Bibhása (2nd, in the first table) :—

1 3 1 3 5 3 5 8 8 10 13 13 10 8 10 8
S R S R, G R G P, P Dh S S, Dh P Dh P,

10 8 5 8 10 8 5 3 5 3 5 3 1
Dh P G P, Dh P G R, G R G R, S.

Bindra'bani-Sa'rang (4th in the first table) :—

1 3 6 8 6 3 3 6 8 8 11 13 13 11
S R M P, M R R M, P P K-N S, S K-N

8 11 8 6 3 6 3 6 3 1
P K-N, P M R M, R M R S.

Bana'gli (7th in the first table) :—

1 5 6 8 6 5 6 8 11 8 11 13 13 11
S G M P, M G M P, K-N P K-N S, S K-N

8 6 5 5 6 8 6 8 6 5 1
P M, G G M P, M P M G, S.

Jogi or Jilha'-Bhairvi (27th in the first table) :—

1 2 4 6 6 8 9 8 8 9 11 13 13 11
S K-R K-G M, M P K-Dh P, P K-Dh K-N S, S K-N

9 8 9 8 6 4 6 4 2 2 1
K-Dh P, K-Dh P M K-G, M K-G K-R K-R, S.

Kalya'na (39th in the first table) :—

1 3 5 3 5 7 8 8 10 12 10 12 13 13 12
S R G R, G T-M P P, Dh N Dh N, S S N

10 8 10 8 7 5 5 3 1
Dh, P Dh P T-M, G G R S.

Alaia'-Bila'val (6th in the second table) :—

1 3 5 8 10 11 12 13 13 12 11 10 8
S R G P, Dh K-N N S, S N K-N Dh, P

10 11 10 10 8 6 5 3 5 8 6 5 5 3 1
Dh K-N Dh, Dh P M G, R G P M, G G R S.

Goud-Sa'rang (6th in the third table) :—

1 3 6 5 5 7 8 8 3 1 1 3 6 5 5
S R M G, G T-M P P, R S S R, M G G

7 8 8 10 12 10 12 13 13 12 10
T-M, P P Dh N, Dh N S S, N Dh

8 3 6 5 8 3 1
P R, M G P R, S.

The above extensions, which are purposely made most simple, and without regard for Tála (time), strictly preserve the principle of ascent and descent, and show a way as to how Rágas can be extended. It is not necessary to stick to the above formations. Any formations, with due regard to the principle of ascent and descent, would do as well. As there is a legitimate liberty in the Poetry to slightly disregard the Grammar, so is the case with the Rágas in their extensions.

We give below a common formation of some of the Rágas by Minḍ or Ghasiṭ, to show how an artistic formation is effected. The formations are not set to Tála (time).

Bhupa or Bibhása (2nd in the first table) :—

1 3 5 3 5 8 5 3 5 8 10 13 13 10 8 5
S R-G R, G-P-G R, G P-Dh S, S-Dh-P G,

3 5 3 1
R-G-R S.

Darbári Kánaḍá (35th in the first Table) :—

1 3 3 4 3 4 6 8 9 11 13 13 11
S R R-K-G, R-K-G-M-P, P-K-Dh-K-N-S, S K-N

9 11 9 8 6 8 8 6 6 4 3 4 3
K-Dh-K-N, K-Dh-P M-P, P-M M-K-G, R-K-G-R

1
S.—(This Ra'ga, if deprived of its Minds or Ghasits, will be reduced to Jilha'-Sind-Bhairvi. We shall speak of this subject in its proper place).

Desa (10th in the second table) :—

1	3 6 5 3	3 6 8	8 10 12 13	13	12	10	8	6
S	R-M-G,-R	R-M-P,	P Dh-N-S,	S	N	Dh	P,	M

5	3 6	6 5	3 1
G	R-M,	M-G	R S.

The above three formations of Bhupa or Bibha'sa, of Darbári-Kanaḍá, and of Desa, if reproduced either by voice or by instruments, will give us an idea, though not a complete one, as to how an artistic performance of the Minḍ or Ghasiṭ is effected.

The artistic execution of Rágas belongs more to the domain of the art than to the subject of this discussion. However, a carefnl study of the above formations, along with their preceding and succeeding dlscussion with a little knowledge of the art, will show a way to extend, to adorn, and to set to music any Rága. As a matter of fact no Rága is complete without its Murchhanás being touched by Minḍ or Ghasiṭ.

It is superfluous to say that all Rágas admit of being extended, though in different degrees, on account of their difference in the number of Notes which they (Ra'gas) cover. This extension is called Prastára,

When they touch a Note or Notes and its or their corresponding Note or Notes in the octaves, one below (Anudátt), or one above (Udátt) the register (Svaritt) octave, they call the touching in the register octave Vádi, and in the other two octaves Samvádi, for instance, in Kalyána (39th in the first table) :—

Samváḍi Below or Anudátt.			Vádi, Register or Svaritt.			Samvádi. Above or Udátt.		
1	3	5	1	3	5	1	3	5
S	R	G.	S	R	G	S	R	G

Samvádi Below or Anudátt			Vádi, Register or Svaritt			Samaàdi Above or Uda'tt		
7	8	10	7	8	10	7	8	10
T-M	P	Dh.	Γ-M	P	Dh,	T-M	P	Dh.

Instead of touching the corresponding Note of a Rága in the other two octaves, they touch other Notes of the same Rága in the said octaves. This process goes by the same of Anuvádi, for example, in Kalyana (39th in the first table) ;—

Anuvádi. Below or Anudutt.			Vádi. Register or Svaritt.			Anuvadi. Above or Udátt.		
7	8	10	1	3	5	7	8	10
T-M	P	Dh.	S	R	G	T-M	P	Dh.

It is not compulsory to touch first Va'di, and then Samvádi and thence Anuva'di, but any arrangement with due regard to the principle of ascent and descent, will be acceptable. It is also not necessary to touch the equal numbers of Va'di, Samvadi, and of Anuvadi, for instance, in Kalyàna (39th in the first table) :—

Anuvádi. Below or Anuda'tt.				Vádi. Register or Svaritt.			Samvádi. Above or Udátt.					
7	8	10	12	1	3	5	1	3	8	5	7	8
T-M	P	Dh.	N.	S	R	G.	S	R	G	T-M	P	

It is hardly necessary to say that Va'di, Samva'di, and Anuvadi are not only touched in simple jumping, but, also, in Minḍ or Ghasiṭ, and seldom in Murki. A Selection of the Viva'di for a Ràga, is condemned and discarded, as most unmusical, for instance in Kalya'na (39th in the first table) :—

Vivádi. Below or Anudátt.			Vádi. Register or Svaritt.			Vivádi. Above or Udátt.		
2	6	9	1	3	5	2	4	7
K-R	M	K-Dh.	S	R	G.	K-R	K-G	T-M,
2	3	4	7	8	10	4	7	9
K-R	R	G.	T-M	P	Dh.	K-G	T-M	K-Dh,

The subject of Va'di, Samva'di, Anuva'di, and of Viva'di, is a controversial one. There are some who say that the Vádi, Samva'di, Anuvadi, and Viva'di are the names given to the Notes of Ràgas according to their (Notes') relative arrangement, and, therefore, they have nothing to do with the change of octaves. But as we are not guided exclusively by the musical scriptures, we need not discuss anything that is vague and meaningless. If the Va'di, Samvadi, and Anuva'di do not imply the change of octaves, then what do they signify ? The word Viva'di only shows that a certain arrangement of the Notes is not thought to be acceptable even by a change of octaves, as it (Viva'di) creates inartistic or unæsthetic effect. We have found the true meaning of the subject in practice, which is an ample and reasonable justification for our view of the matter.

The definition—(which is generally accepted) ot the three Gra'mas, namely, Shaḍja, Madhyam, and Pancham, and of their respective names—Nandyá-Vratt (Nandi is an emblem of the earth), Subhadra (very good or higher), and Jimuta (cloud hence celestial)—is too unintelligible or fabulous to be of any use in this discussion. The definitions of Bhoga, Abhoga, and Samsthái or Sancha'i are more hair-splitting than descriptive, and we omit them as such from this discussion.

It is certainly more charming than pleasant (for the practised ear) to listen to distinct Ra gas clearly preserved by strictiy confiniug to the uumber of Notes and to the rigid but distinctive principle of ascent and descent. This principle along with others, admirably preserves the individual Rágas and prevents confounding one with the other.

The confusion of Rágas invariably generates (in the practised ear) a chaotic group (like the Vivádi) of Notes, however skilful and regular in time they (Notes) may be. It is a truism that with the increase of progress in music, the number of Rágas must necessarily be increased, but it is also true that the increase in the number of Rágas involves definiteness of the distinctive signs. The number of Rágas in recent times, has not been increased, but it has been decreased. Increase, if there is any, has partly been on the side of Chijas (poetry set to music) in a Rága, and wholly on the side of Chijas in a Jilhá or Dhun.

Before dismissing this side of our discussion, let us say that one of the most artistic characteristics of Indian Rágas, is the Murchhaná (literally swoon)—¼th part of a tone.

We have said before [in the second chapter] that the 12 Murchhanás are distributed over all the Rágas, and that they (Murchhanás) are touched only in Minḍ or Ghasiṭ. Now let us add that each Rága consists of two Murchhanás, the first is called "Graha" (literally place), and the second is named "Nyása" (literally distance or interval), and that there is no Murchhaná in a Jilhá or Dhun (diminutive of Rága). This number of Murchhanás in a Rága has admirably been increased in later times not only in the compound Rágas but also in the simple Rágas of Komal-Svaras (semitones) and the effect has simply been charming.

Artistically speaking, simple production of the Notes of a Rága in a given time does not give a complete idea of the Rága so produced, unless its Murchhanás are added to the Notes of which they (Murchhanás) form parts. The Murchhaná is touched first or next to the Note of which it forms a part, and never separately. No stand (pause) is made on a Murchhaná which is never produced without a Mind or Ghasiṭ. If this arrangement is not strictly observed, the Murchhana' will be regarded as a discordant and violently shaky *note*, but that is not the case with it. Artistically speaking, the Murchhana' is a ¼th part of a tone, and it is always produceḍ in Minḍ or Ghasiṭ along with the Note of which it forms a part, and its number is limited in each Ra'ga. There are many Rágas of which the characteristics are the Murchhana's, as distinguishing marks. An omission of the distinctive signs, is the destruction of the Rágas so characterized : this is the reason which confounds Jogia' with Jilha'-Bhairvi (27th in the first table), Darbàri-Kanaḍà with Jilhà-Sind-Bhairvi (35th in the first table), Sáhànà-Kánáḍa with Jilhà-Kàfi (36th in the first table), Sind-Kánaḍá with Jilhá-Sindora (5th in the second table), Jejevanti-Kánaḍa' with Jilha'-Sindora' (5th in the second table), Gándhár with Jilha-Sind-Bhairvi (7th in the second table), Sora'ṭa with Jilha'-Kha'mách (9th in the second table), Palás with Jilhá-Barva' (14th in the second table), Dhanáshri with Jilhá-Ka'fi (15th in the second table), Bhairava with Jilhá-Kálangḍá (18th in the second and 32nd in the first table), Bágeshri-Kánáḍá with Jilhá-Báhár (7th in the third table), and Bhimpalás with Jilhá-Sind Bhairvi (8th in the third table).

The fact of the above confusion simply proves as we have said before, that the Rágas, if deprived of their Murchhana's, and of their principle of ascent and descent, result in Dhuns (not complete) or Jilha's of those Ra'gas : this is the reason why Jilha' or Dhun is recognized as diminutive of Ra'ga, for the former is not so distinctive as the latter. It is hardly necessary to say that even the touching of the Notes of a Ra'ga with Minḍ or Ghasiṭ, without covering its Murchhana's, results in Dhun of that Ra'ga. When the production of Notes of a Ra'ga, is devoid of Minḍ or Ghasiṭ, it results in a simple Jilha' or jumping. It is not to be understood that by implication we disparage simple jumping of the Notes, which has its own charms. We have used the word

" Jumping" simply as opposed to the Minḍ or Ghasiṭ which means connection. Even in a complete form of a Ra'ga, we do not encumber each and every Note of it with Minḍ or Ghasiṭ and Murchhana'; if we want to have the music of that Ra'ga, and not to have an impracticable, if not an impossible, feat. If the Murki, trill, shake, and other principles adorn the Notes, the Minḍ or Ghasiṭ, and the Murchhana' do the same thing, if not more.

To render the above facts clear, we give below the 12 Murchhana's with the 12 Notes (Chromatic scale) on which they (Murchhana's) depend. The Murchhana's are the chief if not the only, item of Indian Raga's, and they are also called Tartivra (double sharp or sharper) or Ati-Komal (double flat or very flat). There is another minuter but none the less perceptible division of the Murchhana', but as it comes under the principle of shaking, we need not treat it separately. In shaking a Note the action, however skilful it may be, is always either of raising or of lowering a Note, but generally the former. The artistic way of shaking a Note cannot be called discordant and violent.

Instead of showing the utility of the Murchhana' (¼th part of a tone) we simply quote the following paragraphs.

P. Blaserna says :—" Certain notes adopted by the Greeks at a period of decline—as, for example, quarter tones—are decisively rejected by us. It is therefore an error which many commit, to think that music, and especially modern music, has absolute character and values, and therefore to reject every musical system which does not agree with ours. There is nothing absolute in it but the laws of notes and their combinations, but the application of these laws is rather vague, and there remains a very wide and indeterminate field, which will be traversed in very different ways by different nations at various historical epochs."

* * * "It may be well believed that even twenty-four keys well arranged would not offer insurmountable difficulties of execution, and even if musical complications and arabesques had to be abandoned, true aud serious music would only be the gainer."

Helmholtz, in suggesting some reforms in the temperate scale, says :—" That by starting from somewhat different considerations, it is possible to provide for everything in a very satisfactory manner, with twenty-four notes per octave."

Instead of giving a table to show the 12 Notes (Chromatic) on which the 12 Murchhanás (¼th part of a tone) depend, we simply say that the first Murchhaná is between S (C) and K-R (C Sh.), the second stands between K-R (C Sh.) and R (D), the third between R (D) and K-G (D Sh.), the fourth is between K-G (D Sh.) and G (E), and so on. According to this arrangement, the first Murchhaná is between S (C) and K-R (C Sh.), and the 12th between N (B) and S (C).

The above description shows that to produce a Murchhaná in a Minḍ or Ghasiṭ we must touch the Note on which it depends. If we want to produce, for instance, the first Murchhanà, we can do it only by two ways – first, we may touch the Note S(C) and then the Murchhaná, or we may touch first the K-R (C Sh. or D Fl.) from the S (C) and then the Murchhaná. It is hardly necessary here to remind ourselves that to touch the S (C) by a Minḍ or Ghasiṭ, we must go first to N (B) or to K-N (B Fl. or a Sh.) to Dh (A) or to K-Dh (A Fl. or G Sh.), as the case may be, for we know that there are Rágas from which the three Notes—N (B), K N (B Fl. or A Sh.), and Dh (A) are excluded, as in the cases of Bibhása (1st in the first table) and Rámkali or Gunkali (11th in the first table).

What does an artist do when he wants to touch the first Murchhanà, which is a Murchhaná of Purvi and such other Rágas ? He first touches the Note S (C) from N (B) or from any other Note, as it suits his convenience, then the Murchhaná, and thence the

K-R (D Fl.), and finally he reverts to the S (tonic); or he goes first to the K-R (C Sh.) from S (C) and then the Murchhanà, before reverting to the S (C).

In showing the second Murchhaná, which is a Murchhaná of Bibhàsa and such other Rágas, the performer gives the Murchhaná first, and then the K-R (D Fl), on the reverse. The third Murchhanà is a Murchhaná of Sárangs and such other Ra'gas. Instead of swelling the body of this discussion, we give below the Ra'gas according to the order of the number of Murchhana' which they possess for their first Murchhana', and the number of their second Murchhana' is given at the end of each name.

Ra'gas with the first Murchhana', are :—Jaita 8th, Puria' or Renki 7th, Ma'rva' or Dipak 7th, Purvi 8th, Dipak or Purvi-Kalya'na 8th, Shri 8th, Jaita'shri 8th, Ma'lava 8th and Purvi-Hindi 8th.

Ra'gas with the 2nd Murchhana', are :—Bibha'sa 9th, Ra'mkali or Gunkali 9th, Lalat 9th, Lalita' or Lalat 10th, Jogia 9th, Gurjari 9th, Toḍi 9th, Sohini 9th, Basant 10th, Paraja 9th, Jogia' 9th, and Bhairava 9th.

Ra'gas with the third Murchhana's, are :—Bhupa or Bibha'sa 10th, Megh or Sur-Malha'r 10th, Brinda'-bani-Sa'rang 11th, Sur-Sa'rang 12th, Baḍhans-Sarang 10th, Madhuma't- Sa'rang 12th, Bila'val 10th, Ra'ma-da'shi-Sarang 10th, Ala'ia-Bilaval 10th, Desha'si 10th, Suraṭa 10th, Desa 10th, Gounḍ 10th, Miaki or Ta'na-sen's Malhár 10th (Ta'nsen's Malhar is wonderfully finished for its Murchhana's. It has the Murchhana's of Megh or Sur-Malha'r, of Ka'naḍa's and of other Ra'gas. Whoever hears this Ra'ga, in its true form, will have an idea as to the wonderful gift of the cele-brated singer for composing Ra'gas), Gounḍ-Malha'r 10th, and Gouḍ-Sa'rang 10th

Ra'gas with the fourth Murchhana', are :—Ma'lkosa 11th, Koushi 11th, Na'yaki-Ka'naḍa' 11th, Madhur-Ka'naḍa' 12th, Darba'ri-Ka'naḍa'11th, Sa'ha'ná-Kánaḍá 11th, Dha'ni-Ka'naḍa 12th, Sind-Ka'naḍa' 11th, Jeje-vanti-Ka'naḍa'11th, Gandha'r 11th, Pala's 11th, Dhana'-

shri 11th, Jounpuri 12th, Multa'ni 12th, Ba'geshri-
Ka'naḍa' 11th, and Bhimpala's 11th.

Ra'gas with the fifth Murchhana', are :—Ba'nga'li
11th, Tilanga or Banga'li 12td, Ma'leshri 12th, Hindola
12th, Bhupa'li 12th, Khamba'bati 11th, Deshi 12th,
Ṭankika' 12th, Pancham 12th, Jangala' 12th, Kalya'na
12th, Khama'cha 11th, Biha'ga 12th, Shankara' 12th,
Shankara'-Bharan 12th, Yaman-Kalya'na 12th, Ha'mir
12th, Na'ṭa 12th, and Chha'ya' 12th.

Ra'gas with the sixth Murchhana' are :—Ka'moda
12th, Biha'gaḍa' 12th, and Keda'ra' 12th.

Ka'langḍa' is a Jilha', and, therefore, it has no Murchhana'.

Without dilating on the distribution of the 12
Murchhana's, suffice it to say that with the progress
of Mind or Ghasiṭ the touching of the Murchhana's
is marvellously developed. Even in a simple Ra'ga',
the number of the Murchhana's is increased. This
increase in Murchhana's in a Ra'ga, is in proportion
to the number of the Komal-Svaras (semitones)
which that Ra'ga covers.

We give below a common formatiou, without Ta'la
(time), of Kalya'na (39th in the first table) to show
how the two Murchhana's of it are covered, It is
hardly necessary to say that the Murchhana' is a ¼th
part of a tone, and it is produced only in a Mind or
Ghasiṭ, and no stand (pause) is made on it.

```
1 3 5   3 5      3 5   7    8  8  10
S R G,  R—G-¼---R—G—T-M—P,  P  Dh.
```

```
10  12     10  12 13 13 12 10 10  8
Dh—N-¼-----Dh--N—S  S,   N—Dh Dh—--P,
```

```
7 · 5   5 3 1
T-M  G,  G—R—S,
```

The above formation, which is an ordinary piece
for an artistic singer or player of Joḍ-music, may

not be reproduced either by voice or by instrument by a novice without a long practice. Therefore, we do not wish to treat the subject of Murchhanás further. However, in concluding the subject we say, as we have said before, that with the progrsss in Minḍ or Ghasiṭ the number of Murchhana's is increased in a Rags of Komal-Svaras (Semitones) ; for instance, in Kalya'na (39th in the first table) there is a room for a third Murchhana' between Tivra-Madhyam (F Sh. or G Fl.) and Pancham (G), aad the number of the third Murchhana', is 7. In an artistic performance of a Ra'ga, the artist does not show a Murchhana' only once, but at a stretch he shows the Murchhana' along with the Note on which it depends, more than once, and the effect, thus produced, is simply entrancing. When a Minḍ or Ghasiṭ does not show a Murchhana', it goes by the name of Khaḍi, and when it shows it, it is called Suda.

Now is the proper time to say that each Ra'ga has certain Notes as its Pradha'na or Pramukha (principal) on which a comparatively long stand is made. This snbject is exclusively an artistic one, and, therefore, we should not pass it over without speaking a word concerning it.

Those who are practised to the Ra gas give a preponderance to certain Notes, which are the principal (ornamental) Notes of that Ra'ga, and its remaining Notes are thought to be subordinate ones.

Apart from the artistic considerations, the object of selecting particular Notes to make a stand on, seems to be that when many Ra'gas blend with each other considerably there must be as many distinctive marks as possible, and the subject of "Pradha'na" is one of them.

As a general guidance, we say that the principal Notes of a Ra'ga are generally the Notes, on which the Murchhana's of that Ra'ga depend.

Before dismissing this side of our discussion, let us mention that there is a custom of long standing to sing or play particular Ra'gas at particular time of the day and night. This custom has got such a stronghold over the mind of those who are practised to the Indian Ra′gas, that a departure from it is regarded by them as most unseasonable and unenjoyable. But the above analysis, though not a scientific one, does not support the custom. Nor does it seem to be warranted by any intrinsic influence of musical sounds. Neither does it seem to be justifiable on the ground of any distinctive Note or Notes which go to form the above Ra′gas. The most that can be brought forward to maintain the conventionality, is that there are certain Ra′gas—such as Bhairava and Sur-Sa′rang, Jogia and Megh, Toḍi and Gounḍ-Malha′r, Puria′ and Gouḍ-Sa′rang, Sohini and Desa, Lalit and Kalya′na, &c., &c.—which are distinct from each other in Murchhana′s, in tones and in semitones, and which above all produce different efforts on account of their different formations. But difference in impression does not follow difference in time. If it is assumed that the effect produced by Bhairva, Jogia, Toḍi, Puria′, Lalat and by such other Ra′gas, is softer or less excitable or less lively than the one produced by Sa′rangs, Ka′naḍa′s, Malha′rs, Kalya′ns and such other Ra′gas, still liveliness or dullness has nothing whatever to do with any particular time in itself. It cannot be presumed that a particular time of the day or night by itself changes pleasureable feelings into painful ones, or *vice versa*.

In order to sing or play any Ra′ga at any time and to thereby break through the ancient custom, many old celebrities seem to have mixed, more ingeniously than musically, two Ra′gas of quite different melodies, such as Hindola-Ba′ha′r, Bhairava-Ba′har—otherwise called Pancham (not of our table), and many others, and they have called others by misnomers, such as Gouḍ-Sa′rang, Ra′tki-Puria, Dinki-Puria′, Kukab-Bilaval, Sarfarda′-Bilavala, &c,

Instead of refuting the so-called theory of a particular Ra′ga for a particular time at length and of bringing forth good many arguments against it, we may challenge any advocate of the custom to reasonably explain, out of many instances, why "Toḍi" (29th in the first table) is fixed for the *morning* and why "Multa'ni" (17th in the second table) is meant only for the *afternoon* ?

It is sheer madness to think that the Toḍi shows any sign of the diurnal revolution of the earth, and when its second Note (C Sh.) is omitted only in ascent, which is done in the case of Multa'ni, it shows the mean or extreme difference from 6 to 8 hours chronometrically. These remarks are equally applicable to the *Season-Ra'gas.*

To speak anything in abstract concerning Time is to leap into "mystery" which H. Spencer describes thus :—"It results therefore that Space and Time are wholly incomprehensible. The immediate knowledge which we seem to have of them, proves, when examined, to be total ignorance. While our belief in their objective reality is insurmountable, we are unable to give any rational account of it. And to posit the alternative belief (possible to state but impossible to realize) is to multiply irrationalities."

To realize time (Ta'la) in concrete is to experience "rhythm" or pulsation which is a marked distinction of music, and as such we treat it in the next chapter.

IV

THE TA'LAS AND THEIR FORMATIONS

A. Bain says :—"In his very subtle and original analysis, Sully traces the attribute of unity in variety through all the various guises assumed in musical compositions. First and most conspicuous, as a means of unity, is Time. To make a sequence of tone all equal in time, gives the simplest impression of unity, in variety. Next is a sequence where the tones are alternated with their sub-divisions—a semibreve with two crotchets, and so on. This is carried up to the Foot or Bar, which confers on music its distinguishing rhythmic character, as triple, quadruple, &c."

Tála (Time-measures), which is an important factor of every school of music (even barbarian vociferation), regulates the relative durations of musical sounds, and as such seems to have considerably engrossed the Indian mind.

That which the Indians call Mátrá (metre), is an unit of Tála. For the sake of simplification, we call 1, 2, 3, 4, 5, 6, 7, 8, 9, &c, when counted or pronounced at a regular and uniform interval ("Laya"), as Mátrás. Tála is an aggregate of the Mátrás or equal lengths of a piece of music. The number of Mátrás in each Tála is fixed. If we repeat the figure 1 (one) and adjust a stroke either by the hands, or by any other means with the first letter of the word one, we get A'ditála (primary), which is ordinarily known by the name of Dádrá (literally ladder). The A'ditála is the foundation on which other Tálas are based. If we repeat 1, 2, and strike only at the first letter of the word one, we get Jhaptála. In repeating 1, 2, 3, and striking the first letter of the word one, we get Gajaltála or Dipchandi (practically, this is like a treble and it is used extensively). In repeating 1, 2, 3, and striking the first letters of the words one and two, we realize Rupaktála (this Tála also covers 3½ Mátrás and called Jhampá). Before going further, we must say that in order to increase the number of Mátrás in a Tála, they have called them by the name of Avasána, of tála, and of kála (rest). The first (Avasán) is the beginning or end of a Tála, and it is also the point of meeting of musicians and drummers—and of receiving applause from audience. The second is the point of a stroke (tála), and the third is that of an absence of strokc (rest).

When a Tála is repeated, each repetition is called Avarda', correction of A'vritti (repetition). A number of repetitions does not changc a Ta'la, bnt it shows the number of repetitions.

In Jhapta'la, Gajaltála or Dipchandi, and in Rupaktala the point of Avasána is not a tála (stroke), but a kála (rest). No cause is shown for this deviation.

To simplify our immediate subject in hand, we allot the Avasána (storke)—otherwise called "Sama" —the *first place* in the seriál order of tne Mátrás in a Tála. We give a *serial figure* to the tála (stroke, but not the Avasána) which is called "Bhari" (not empty). We show the kála (rest)—otherwise called "Khāli" (empty)—by a serial *figure in a bracket*. This process at once teaches us that the first figure stands for the Avasána, the figure without a bracket, is the sign of tála, and the figure in a bracket, is the mark of kála.

If we go by the above method, we reproduce the Titála or Tirvaṭtála (4 Mátrás, but 3 strokes) in the following way :—

1, 2, (3), 4. Here are the Surfáktála (5 Mátrás, but 3 strokes)—1, (2), 3, 4, (5), Choutála or Ekká (6 Mátrás, but 4 strokes)—1, (2), 3, (4), 5, 6, and A'ḍa'chouta'la (7 Ma'tra s, but 4 strokes)—1, 2, (3), 4, (5), 6, (7).

The above Ta'las are thc principal ones, and others are their specializations. The special Ta'las arc effected simply by doubling or quadrupling the number of Ma'tra's of the original Tálas and by simply changing the order of strokes and rests. For example, the Dhamàr or Hori (difficult and seldom practised: its Avasàna is not on a stroke) is neither more nor less than the A'ḍáchoutála doubled, and its strockes and rests changed.

A'ḍàchoutála—1, 2, (3), 4, (5), 6, (7).

Dhama'r—1, (2), (3), (4), (5), 6, (7), (8), (9), (10), 11, (12), (13), (14).

The big-named Brahmatála and Rudratála are no other Tálas than the Titála and Surfa'kta'la quardrupled, and their order of strokes and rests changed.

Tita'la— 1, 2, .(3),
Brahmta'la—1, (2), 3, (4), 5, (6), 7, 8, (9), 10, 11, 12,
4.
(13), 14, 15, I.

Surfa'kta'la - (*figs. 1st & 3rd lines*)
1, 2, 3,
Rudratála—1, (2), 3, (4), 5, 6, (7), 8, 9, 10, (11), 12, 13,
4, (5)
14, 15, (16), 17, 18, 19, 20.

The Savàritála or Kaid (literally hampered) is no other Tála than the Titála, but the real Savári is not used now. It has 7 Mátrás and a half, and this is the reason why it is difficult. This Savári when doubled and its strokes and rests changed, goes by the name of Brahmatála (another form of the original Brahmatála).

Savàritála—1, 2, (3), 4, (5), 6,
Brahmtála—1, (2), 3, (4), 5, (6), 7, 8, (9), 10, 11,(12),
(7), ($\frac{1}{2}$).
13, 14, 15.

The peculiarity of Tála is that instead of going at a regular interval (Laya), the singer or player in competing with the drummer at times changes the point of Avasán to ½ or ¼ of that Mátrá. The former is called A'ghát or Atit (no stroke), and the latter is named Anughát (after the stroke).

To break up the monotony or the dead uniformity of time, the singer or player (who deals more with simple jumping than with Minḍ or Ghasiṭ and Murki) at times, reduces the original time (Barobari) or speed to one-half (Ṭha'), or at times he doubles (Dviguni or Duni) it, or quadruples (Chougun) it. And, as a matter of course, the drummer adopts the same course. Thá (one-half), Barobari (equal), Duni (double), and Chougun (quadruple) are the relative terms, and their relation to each other stands thus :—

Thá is equal to a Semibreve, Barobari is equal to a Minim, Duni is equal to a Crotchet, and Chougun is equal to a Quaver ; or in other words, Thá is equal to 8 Annas, Barobari is equal to 16 Annas, Duni is equal to 32 Annas, and Chougun is equal to 64 Annas or equal parts of a Rupee. Thay also double the Chougun in Tàn (variation), but they never go further than this ; or in other words, they use a semi-quaver, but not a demisemi-quaver.

They at times accelerate the original time (Barobari) or speed to 1½ (A'ḍa or Deḍi), or to 1¼ (Kuáḍa or Savái), but this is very difficult. To realize this difficulty we suggest to our readers an attempt to produce instantaneously with the hands—Titála with Choutála (A'ḍa or 1½) and Tita'la with Surfa'kta'la (Kua'ḍa or 1¼) ; or in other words, the Tita'la and Chouta'la and Tita'la and Surfa'kta'la should be regulated in such a way as to converge their respective Avasa'ns. This attempt is sure to be attended with an abnormal difficulty in the absence of a key, which we have invented and have given at the end of the description of Ta'las.

Indians seem to have taken great pains to form the technical vocabulary of their drumming, as an art. The peculiarity of Indian Pakha'vaja (Paksha-A'va'ja means sounded by two sides) or Tabla'-Ba'ya' (detached Pakhavaja), is that it is generally attuned (few drummers know how to adjust it completely) to the fundamental (Svaritt) note - S (C or tonic) of the musicians. It is played by the palms and fingers of both the hands at the edge, at the middle, and on the centre of the two circles into which it is divided. The right-hand side (not of a left-handed drummer), which is besmeared with iron to make it resonant, is called Daina' or Dakshan ; and the left-hand side, which is also made resonant by pressing it with wheat-flour to adjust it with the right side, is called B'ya' or Va'ma. The instrument (artistic excluded) is too common and noisy to need any description. The right-hand fingers are used more freely than those of the left hand. The stroke, which is produced in the middle of the right side by the right palm, is named Ta'l ; and the stroke by the same palm on the centre (iron), is called Ti or Tin, The stroke, which is produced at the edge by the index finger of the right hand, goes by the name of Na'. The similar (four fingers, excepting the thumb) arrangement, if manipulated by the left hand on the left side, is named Ga, Ghi or Ghin, and Ka respectively. When the right palm and the left-hand fingers produce a stroke jointly in the middle of their respective circles, the stroke thus produced goes by the name of Dha'—the usual, but not an invariable, sign of the Avasa'na. It is not necessary to say that the Dha' is a compound stroke of the Ta' and Ga. A compound stroke of the Ti or Tin and Ghin, is named Dhin. This arrangement is slightly changed on Tabla'-Ba'ya' (detached Pakha'vaja. There is but very little difference between Pakha'vaja and Tabla'-Ba'ya' instrumentally. The former is handled more with the palms and the joint fingers of the left hand (sometimes only three fingers, excepting the thumb and the last, are used separately) than with separate fingers of the hands ; while the latter is played more by the fingers than by the palms, and even the left-hand fingers (three excepting the thumb and the last) are used more freely and separately. Pakhavaja is generally played with Dhrupada and Dhama'r (music set to Dhama'rta'la), and Tabla'ba'ya' regulates (not in Madras) the Khya'l, Ṭappa', Ṭhumri, Gazal and Dance.

By adjusting the palms and the fingers at different points on the right and left sides of Pakhavaja or Tabla'-ba'ya', we get in all (artistic and practical drumming) 13 letters or technicalities as elements composing the Ṭheka's and Parands (we shall speak of these in their proper place), which are played in accompaniment of music. The letters are these :—

Ka, Ga, Gha, Ṭa, Ḍa, Ta, Tha, Da, Dha, Na, Ma, Ra, and La (the last is obsolete).

A combination of the above letters, is formed thus :—1st.—Ka or Ka' Kḍa'n, Kiṭ and Kiḍ.
2nd.—Ga or Gi, Gan and Gadi or Gdi.
3rd.—Ghḍa'n, Ghiṭ, Ghiḍ, and Ghin.
4th.—Ta or Ta', Ti or Tu, Tak, Tag, Tiṭ, Tin or Tun, Tir and Ṭra'n.
5th.—Tho and Thun.
6th.—Di and Dag or Dig.
7th.—Dha or Dha', Dhḍa'n, Dhig, Dhiṭ, Dhiḍ, Dhin, Dhir, Dhla'ng (obsolete), and Dhum.
8th—Na or Na', Nak, or Nag.

The one Ma'tra' combinations (or monosyllables), which are given above, show that out of the 12 (13th is absolete) letters 8 are used as initial as well as final (Ghi is not final), and the remaining four (Ṭ, Ḍ, M and R.) are used only as final. The ways in which the above combinations are made, and the addition of nasal sounds—M and N (in Kḍa'n, Gan, Gha'ḍn, Ghin, Tin, Tra'n, Thun, Dha'ḍn, Dhin, Dhum, &c.) only in pronouncing and not in playing, and the substitution of R for Ḍ (in Tra'n and not Tḍa'n) in pronounciug and not in playing seem to be either arbitrary, or probably they are a modification or a part of the 14 Sutras, which are attributed to Siva thus—" (Siva) The King of Kings of musicians

(" Nata ") in order to gratify the desire of Sanaka and other Rishis (sages) played fourteen times on the Ḍamaru when he was in an elevated state of feeling (Nritya or dancing) and these collections are known as Shiva Sutras." The 14 Sutras, for our purpose, are tolerably these :—

1st. A I Un, 2nd. Ri Lrik, 3rd. E On, 4th. Ai Auch, 5th. Ha'ya Vara'ṭa, 6th. Lana, 7th. Yaman Nanam, 8th. Zabha Ghaḍ Dhak, 9th. Jab Gaḍ Dash, 10th. Khap Chhaṭ Tha,. 11th. Chaṭ Tav, 12th. Ka Pain, 13th. Shakh Sar, and the 14th. Hal.

We shall be wanting in doing justice to our discussion if we do not speak a word about the "Damaru," which is said to have been used as an instrument to produce the 14 Sutras. With due respect to the Sutras, we are most painfully constrained to say that the " Damaru," which we know, and which is played by our aboriginal tribes or brothers with a stick and a little pressure by a few fingers of the left hand, is a primitive form of the advanced Pakha'-vaja of our day. We cannot bring ourselves to believe that the Damaru can admit of so admirable Sutras, which are said to be the fundamental basis of Aryan philosophy aud religion. But as this subject is a religious one, we leave it to abler heads and religious hearts, more especially as it in no way furthers our discussion. What little we have said concerning the " Damaru " should not be interpreted into an indirect attack on the Sutras. In tracing the identity or origin of the drum technicalities, we have touched the " Damaru " only in passing.

As we have given one Mátra' combinations, we give now two Ma'tra' combinations to show how they are formed in Theka's and Parands, which are extant :—

1st.—Ka-Ta', Ka-Dha', Kḍa'n-Ta', Kḍa'n-Dha', Kiṭ-Ta, Kiḍ-Tak, Kiṭ-Thun, Kiḍ-Dhum, Kiḍ-Na' and Kid-Na'g.

2nd.—Ga-Ta', Ga-Ḍhá, Ga-Dhin, and Gdi-Gan or Gadi-Gan,

3rd.—Ghiṭ-Tak, Ghiḍ-Tit, Ghiḍ-Nag, Ghḍa'n-Ta', Ghḍa'n-Dha', and Ghiṭ-Thun,
4th.—Ta-Kiṭ, Ta'-Thun, Tag-Tiṭ, and Tir-Kiṭ.
5th.—Tho-Kiṭ, Thun Ga', Thun-Ta', Thun-Thun, Thun-Dha', and Thun-Na'.
6th.—Dig-Ta', Dig-Dhá, and Dig-Nag.
7th.—Dha-Kiṭ, Dhá-Tiṭ, Dhig-Nag, Dhir-Kiṭ, Dhi-Láng (obsolete), and Dhum-Kiṭ.
8th.—Na-Kiṭ, Nag-Tiṭ, Nag-Dhiṭ, Nag-Thun, Nag-Dhun or Dhum.

When the above combinations are given the same time, which is given to the proceding ones (one Mátrá combinations), the speed ("Laya") will be relatively double (Duni).

There are certain other combinations, but we have selected the best according to our taste of drumming, and they also serve as specimens. The beauty of a combination is that it not only sounds well, but it admits of being played swiftly with comparative ease. In short, the above technicalities and their combinations are so exquisitely formed in different divisions of Tála, and they are played so smoothly and artistically that to become an excellent drummer would require a life-long practice. Mathematically Ta'las are of no great consequence, but musically they are of the greatest use.

We give below commonplace Theka's of the principal Ta'las we have spoken of, and also give a few Parands to show how the technicalities are combined. It will be observed that the above specimens and the following combinations, if properly read, will assist us in forming new Theka's and Parands.

The distinction between a Theka' (the word is purely a technical one, literally it signifies contract or license) and a Parand (purely technical), is that the former is a limited and a repeated combination to keep up the Ta'la ; the latter is an extended and generally changed combination to swell (variation in time, that is to say, combinations are not of uniform speed) the Ta'la.

Before giving the Thekás and Parands, it is opportune to say that Pakhávaja deals more in resonant words as Dhá and its combinations, Ghi and its combinations, and Tho and its combinations, than Tablá-báyá which generally deals in Ga and its combinations, Tá and its combinations, Dig and its combinations, and Ná and its combinations. This is in a great measure due to the palms being used more freely in the former than in the latter.

Our reading of the aforsaid combinations, teaches us that " t," when preceded by " i " is always to be pronounced as " ṭ " and not " t." When " d " is preceded either by " i, " or by K, Gh, T, or Dh, it is invariably " ḍ " and not " d." This description may do away with the special letters in the Ṭhekás and Parands by allowing the use of the ordinary ones.

Ṭhekás on Tablá-báyá.

(1), 2.
Jháptála - Ghin Tá Tá, Tin Tá Tá (Avasán on the rest and the first is rest),

1, 2, (3),
Tirvaṭtála—Ná Dhin Dhina, Ná Dhin Dhiná Ná
4.
Tin Tiná, Ná Dhin Dhina'.

1 2, (3), 4,
Tirvaṭ or Tita'la—Dhin Dhin, Dha Tit, Tu Na', Kit Ta',

1, (2), 3, 4,
Surfa'kta'la—Dhin Dhin, Dha' Tit, Tu Na', Ka Tá,
(5).
Kit Ta'.

1, (2), 3,
Ekka' or Chauta'la—Dhin Dhin, Dha' Tit, Tu Na',
(4) 5, 6.
Ka Ta', Dhag Tit, Dhi Na'.

1, 2,
Aḍá (not straight) Chautála—Dhin Dhin, Dhá Tit,
(3) 4, (5) 6, (7),
Tu Na', Ka, Ta' Dhin Dhin, Na' Dhin, Dhin Na'.

1,   2,   (3),

Sava´ri or Kaid—Dhin Ghin, Dha´ Tit, Dhin Ghin

4,   (" ½ "),(5)   6,   (7)

Tuna´ Kata´, Dha´, Dhin Dhin, Na´-Dhin, Na´ Dhin.

If the Dhá (½) is taken away from the Sava´ri it is
reduced to Aḍáchautála in another Theká, and if the
Dhá (½) or its equivalent is added to the A´ḍáchautála
it will serve the purpose of Savári, It is not necessary
to stick to the Thekás which we have given above.
The same Ta´las can be represented by any other
combinations. The object of giving simple Thekàs
with a slight alteration in order to meet the different
Tálas, is to simplify description, and to give an idea
as to how Thekàs are ordinarily composed. There are,
and can be made, excellent Thekás of artistic combi-
tions, but want of space does not permit us to do so.

A peculiar kind of combination, which is familiarly known by the name of A´ḍa, is as follows on
Tablá-báyá :—

1   2   (3)

Tirvaṭ or Titàla—Dhá Ghi Nag, Takit Ghi Nag, Dhà

4   1,   2,

Trak Dhá Kit, Ghi Nag Tin, Ná Gin Ná Gin, Ka

(3)   4

Tak Dhá Kit, Dhá Trak Dhàkit, Ghi Nag Tagan.

Here are common but artistic Parands on Ta'bla´-
báyá,

1.   2,

Tirvaṭ or Titála—Dhinà Kdadhán, Dag Nag Dig

(3)   4   1,

Nag, Tirkît Dag Nag, Dhig Nag Tirkiṭ, Dhag Tit

2   (5)

Tag Tit, Dha´ Trak Dhakit Ghid, Nag Dhit Kit Tak,

4,   1,   2,

Nag Tit Kdán, Dhà Dha´ Dhi Gan, Dha´ Dhi Gan

(3)   4,

Dhà, Kid Nag Tarkit Ṭak Dhir Kit Tak, Dhag Nag
Thag Tiṭ.

1, 2,
Tirvat or Titála—Ta Kit Thunkit Ghid, Nag Dhit
(3) 4, 1,
Kit-Tak, Nag Tit Kdán, Dhá Dhà Dhi Gan, Dhá Dhi
2, (3)
Gan Dhá, Kid Nag Tar Kit Thir Kit Tak, Dhag Nag
4,
Dhag Tit, Dhag Tit Dhag Tit.

Thekàs on Pakha'vaja.—

(1) 2, 3
Rupakta'la—Dha' Dha', Tit Kata', Gadigan. (Avasa'na on rest).
1, 2 (3), 4
Tita'la —Dha' Dha', Dhin Ta, Gadi Gan Dha', Tit Ta'.
1, (2) 3,
Surfa'kta'la—Dha' Dha' Dhin Ta', Gadi Gan Dha',
4, (5)
Dhin Ta', Kit Ta'.
1, (2) 3,
Chauta'la—Dha' Dha', Dhin Tá, Gaḍi Gan Dha',
(4) 5, 6.
Dhin Ta' Tit Ka Ta', Gadi Gan.

The following is a common Theka' for Dhama'r, and a careful perusal of it will show how nicely it is composed.

(1),(2), (3), (4), (5), 6,(7), (8), (9),(10),(11),(12),
Dhamár – Dh——a' Dhi-t Dha' Ga Dhi-n Ti—ta
(13), (14).
T——a' (Avsa'na on rest).

It the Theka's of Tita'la and Surfa'kta'la are quadrupled, they will serve the purpose of Brahmatála and Rudrata'la respectively. When the Theka' of Sava'ri is doubled, it will represent the Brahmatála in other form.

Now we give Parands (common but artistic) on Pakhávaja, which are familiarly known by the name of A'ḍa :—

1, (2),
Chauta'la—Takk Dha' Kit, Ta' Kit Tho Kit,
3, (4), 5,
Dhigan Nagan, Digg Gadi Gan, Katit Dha' Dhin Ta',
6.
Ta' Kit Dha'n.

1, (2), 3,
Chauta'la—Nakit Takit, Katak Dhakit, Dha'n Na'n,
(4), 5, 6.
Dha' Dhinta' Katt, Dhda'n, Nagan Dha'n.

1, (2),
Chauta'la—Dha' Kit Takk, Takk Thokit,
3, (4), 5,
Katt Ghinag, Ka Tit Dha'kit, Nakit Tan,
6.
Kda'n Dha'n.

It is necessary to say that the Dvitt (double) K, G, T and N are accents. Wherever any Dvitt comes, it should be considered as an accent. The accents are beautifully shown in an artistic drumming.

Parands on Pakha'vaja in Chauta'la :—

1, (2), 3, (4),
1st.—Takit Tho, Kit Tak, Dhig Tag, Tag Tit
5, 6, 1, (2),
Ka Tit Ta, Gan Ghi Ghi, Nag Dhigg, Ghda'n
3, (4), 5,
Dhag Na' Na', Kit Takk Thunn, Taka' Thun Thun,
6.
Kit Takk Gadi Gan—(This Parand is in one Avarda', that is to say, in 6 Matra's, but we have given it in two Avarda's, that is in 12 Ma'tra's).

1, (2),
2nd.—Ghin Tir Kit Tak Ta', Ka Ta' Ghi Ghi Dhinn,
3, (4), 5, 6.
Nag Dhitt Ta', Ghin Tda'n Dha', Dhin Ta' Ka Tit,

Dha' Kit Tak Gadi Gan.

1, (2),
3rd.—Dhit Tit Kit Tak, Dhig Tag Tit Ka Ta',
3, (4),
Ghin Tir Kit Tak Tag Tit, Tag Tit Dhag Tit,
5, 6.
Ka Tit Ta Gan Dhag Dhitt, Dhda'n Na Gan Dha'n.
1, (2),
4th.- Dhit Tit Trak Dhit, Dhir Kit Ta' Ghin Dhi Ka
3 (4),
Ta, Kit Tag Tag Tit, Kit Takk Thun Ga' Takk Thun
5, 6.
Ga', Tir Kit Ta. Dhir Kit Ta', Dha Gi Gi Dha Gi Gi.

The few examples given above, though short and not the best, will, however, give an idea as to how the Ṭheka's and Parands are formed. There has been a general belief, and seems to be well-founded, among the Indian musicians that to become an artist one must necessarily and sufficiently appreciate the real beauty of Theka's and Parands as a guide to compose and execute music.

We give below a formula by the aid of which we can easily give out any Ta'la by the left hand and its Duni or double by the right hand at a time. It is unusually difficult to practise this without the support of a process we now speak of. In order to know the formula a few words are necessary :— A stroke by the left hand, should be named—"Ka," and by the right hand—"Ta'." The joint strokes by the left and right hands at a time, should be called—"Dha'," and the absence of a stroke should be signed —"a'." This process teaches us to produce the following Ta'las :—

Tita'la—Dha', Ta', Ka, Ta', Ta', Ta', Ka, Ta'.

Surfa'kta'la—Dha', a', Ta', Ta', Ka, Ta', Ka, Ta', Ta', á.

Chauṭa'la—Dha', a', Ta', a', Dha', Ta', Ta', a', Dha', a', Dha', Ta'.

Aḍa′chauta′la—Dha′, Ta′, Ka, Ta′, a′, Ta′, Ka, Ta, Ta′, a′, Dha′, a′, Ta′, a′.

Instead of giving the strokes and rests, we give below the key which has rendered the process so easy and practical. It is hardly necessary to say that the key will work with all the Ta′las.

Tịta′la—1, 2, (3), 4.
Duni— 1, 2, (3), 4, 1, 2, (3) 4.
Dha′, Ta′, Ka, Ta′, Ta′, Ta′, Ka, Ta′

Surfa′kta′la—1, (2), 3, 4, (5).
Duni—1, (2) 3, 4, (5), 1, (2), 3, 4, (5)
Dha′, a′, Ta′, Ta′, Ka, Ta′, Ka, Ta′, Ta′, a′.

Chauta′la – 1, (2), 3, (4), 5,
Duni—1, (2), 3, (4), 5, 6, 1, (2), 3, (4),
Dha′, a′, Ta′, a′, Dha′, Ta, Ta, a′, Dh a′, a′,
6.
5, 6.
Dha, Ta′.

Aḍa′chauta′la— 1, 2, (3), 4,
Duni—1, 2, (3), 4, (5), 6, (7), 1,
Dha, Ta′ Ka, Ta′, a′, Ta, Ka, Ta′,
(5) 6, (7).
2, (3), 4, (5), 6, (7).
Ta′, a′, Dha′, a′, Ta′, a′.

A careful perusal of the above process shows that when two strokes meet together, we call them Dha′. When there is a stroke on the Duni or double, we term it Ta′; and when there is a stroke on the Ta′la, we name it Ka. It is not necessory to say that "a′" stands for an absence of stroke, and whenever it comes it is always on the Duni or double. The only thing to be done in producing the Ta′las and their Dunis at a time, is to give equal and uniform time ("Laya") to the "signs."

As a novelty, the Chauta'la and Tita'la can be produced by the hands and by a foot at a time in such a way as to converge their (the said Ta'las') respective Avasa'nas. Those who havc seen the way, have admired it much. First, give the Ta'la and Duni of the Chauta'la by the hands as shown above, and adjust the three strokes (rest excluded) of Tita'la by a foot in the following way :—

Hands—Dha', a', Ta', a', Dha', Ta', Ta', a', Dha,
A foot—1, 2, (3),
a', Dha', Ta.
4. (a foot)

In finishing the description of Ta'las we give below, as we have promised, a key by the aid of which Tita'la and Chauta'la (A'ḍa or $1\frac{1}{2}$), and Tita'la and Surfa'kta'la) (Kuaḍa or $1\frac{1}{4}$), can be produced by both the hands at a time in such a way as to converge their respective Avasa'nas.

Suppose we take a series of 12 consecutive figures beginning from 1 and ending with 12. Now in Chauta'la there would be 4 strokes and 2 rests. The strokes will be on 1, 5, 9 and 11 and the rests will be on 3 and 7. The reader must already have seen from the general description that the 1st stroke on 1, is the Avasa'na. In the same manner as regards Tita'la the series will divide itself in 4 points (Ma'tra's) composed of 3 strokes and 1 rest—the strokes coming on 1, 4 and 10, and the rest coming on 7, the stroke on 1 being of course the Avasa'na. The following is a demonstratson of what we are saying :—

Chauta'la—	1,		(2),		3,		(4),		5,		6,	
series—	1,	2,	3,	4,	5,	6,	7,	8,	9,	10,	11,	12
Tita'la—	1,			2,			(3)			4		

The 12 figures are to be counted at a regular and uniform interval and the strokes and rests should be adjusted as shown above.

The above being understood, it is clear that the Titála and Surfákta'la may also be similarly realized.

As the later is $1\frac{1}{4}$ times the former, instead of 12 figures, we shall have to take the series of 20 figures. The result will be that as regards Tita'la there will be strokes on 1, 6 and 16, and the rest on 11 ; and as regards Surfa'kta'la the strokes will be on 1, 9 and 13, and the rests on 5 and 17,

The reader must have seen from the above description and demonstration that the thing to be done, is to take any common multiple of the units (Ma'tra's) contained in the different Ta'las to be produced simultaneously by the hands and their strokes and rests are to be adjusted in the manner aforesaid.

Before dismissing this side of our discussion, it is absolutely necessary to say that we have purposely omitted the subject of giving a mode of setting to the Ta'las the Ra'gas we have spoken of. We cannot do this artistically in the absence of a *notation* of general and recognized acceptance. The ancient notations are too complicated to be clearly understood for a practical purpose, and those which are invented by our present writers on Indian music, are too crude and many to be of general use. We, therefore, strongly recommend our authors to adopt the European *notation* with certain additions to meet the peculiarities of Indian music as a whole. Such a system of *notation* is sure to lay open a way to the advanced music of Europe, and to serve as a channel of exchange.

To secure the above object with least trouble, we must introduce it first in schools and colleges as a means to reduce to writing the music of Indian poems, and it will establish itself in process of time. The dramatists (Náṭakválás) probably be the first to adopt it in their printed programmes and pamphlets (on account of their favourable situation), as a guide to their patrons if they wish to improve their singing,

Our discussion will be incomplete if we do not devote a separate chapter to dancing, as an art, because it is, in its earlier stages (as is the case in barbarian races), co-ordinate with poetry and music., Rhythm in speech, rhythm in sound and rhythm in motion are the elements out of which music or language of emotions or feelings has been evolved. The secret of the great impression which music makes upon the human heart, wholly resides *in rhythmic movements, in determinate intervals, in simple ratios, in rich harmonics, in different sequences and in different shades.*

Spencer says :—"The several kinds of *rhythm*, characterizing æsthetic expression, are not, in the common sense of the word, artificial, but are intenser forms of an undulatory movement habitually generated by feelingin its bodily discharge. It is shown by the fact that they are all traceable in ordinary speech ; which in every sentence has its primary and secondary emphases, and its cadence containing a chief rise aud fall complicated with subordinate rises and falls ; and which is accompanied by a more or less oscillatory action of the limbs when the motion is great."

V

THE THEORY OF DANCING

Dancing, which has all over the civilized world been recognized as an art, is dependent on the muscular action generated by elevated feeling. Feelings are the concomitants of nervous changes. There is a recognized relation between the quantity of feeling (pleasurable or painful) and the amount of motion generated. This mode of expressing emotions, is not performed only by the civilized races, but it is considerably exhibited by birds and animals.

The curious love gestures of some kinds of birds, have remarkably been observed by some naturalists.

Audubon describes thus :—"The males of heron (*audea herodius*) walk about on their long legs with great dignity before the females, and bid defiance to their rivals. With one of the disgusting carron vultures the gesticulations and the parade of the males at the beginning of love season are extremely ludicrous."

Darwin says:—"In Northern America large numbers of grouse meet every morning during the breeding season on a selected level spot, and here they run round and round in a circle of about 15 to 20 feet in diameter, so that the ground is worn quite bare like a fairy-ring. In these partridge dances (called by the hunters) the birds assume the strangest attitudes, and run round and round, some to the left and some to the right. Certain kinds of birds often rise a few feet or yards in the air above some bush, and flutter with a fitful and fantastic motion, singing all the while."

There may be very few of us who have not watched and enjoyey the Chandol (lark), Bulbul (big lark), Dayar and a few other birds undergoing manœuvres of the above description. The dancing of peacock, which is depicted by our poets, is admirable only for the show of its beautiful feathers, and for nothing more.

A. Bain says:—"Next to the experience of Feelings, is the experience of the signs. These are—the recognized expression of human and other sentient beings, by Voice, Movement, Gesture, and Demonstration of every kind."

"Probably the foremost place among the associated signs of feeling should be given to the voice. In the first place, the emission of sound is the most widespread of all the significant signs of the mental states of animals and human beings. Under a stimulation of the senses, as music, our strong favourite emotions are resuscitated ; and the pleasure is a complex product of present sensation and ideal feelings. We, therefore, infer that, when music or other genial stimulation wakens up past occasions of pleasure, these echoes do greatly increase the emotional glow ; and the highly educated emotional man is necessarily much more elated under the circumstance than the poor, the outcast, the emotionally famished man.

"We might carry on the exposition of imitation into all the postures, gesticulations, and motions of the body at large. As regards the lower limbs and the trunk, there is no essential difference from the case already dwelt upon. The feet seem much less prepared originally for varied voluntary movements than the hands ; their accomplishment is both more limited and more laborious, as we see in dancing.

W. D. Whitney says :—"Language is expression for the sake of communication. The instrumentalities capable of being used for this purpose and actually more or less used, are various ; gesture and grimace, pictorial or written signs, and uttered or spoken signs. The first two addressed to the eye, the last to the ear."

It is hardly necessary to say that many of our most important expressions, when exhibited by those who are unhappily born blind, prove that they are innate or not individually learnt. It is strictly true that to perform certain expressive actions in a regular and perfect way, is to imitate and practise them individually.

It is exceedingly regrettable that so natural an expression of delighted feelings,—dancing which is, and has been, manifested by the ideal nations of the world, present and past, has been totally ignored and discarded by ourselves and by our predecssors as a debasing art, and hence its confinement to the female (noble) sex. It is strictly true that the ancient Hindus used to take delight in dancing, not only in religious devotion but in social ceremonies, not only up to the time of Krishna but long after it. Dancing was so much held in reverence by early Hindus that their Sutras were thought to be the result of the dancing of Siva.

Our present dancing, social and professional, though performed by a few male artists, is exclusively feminine. In Madras-dancing there are certain male attributes, but they are so much overpowered by the feminine attributes that we look upon them as exclusively feminine. Social (non-professional) dancing, which is performed in the higher families, and even in the most secluded part of "Zenana" is unsæsthetic. The Rásaḍá, an antiquated name of dancing by males and females, are but now danced by females only. Ladies catch each other's hands as a support, and bow and move round and round in a regulated motion of the feet in a circle, slow in the beginning and fast in the end ; when separated or not supporting each other by the hands, they perform a zig-zag motion, and clap and flourish the hands. Those who possess a sweet voice, take the lead, and others follow in their train. A female drummer or regulator of the voice and of the metre of the feet, sits in the centre. Hámchi (in Guzerat a circle dance and jumping by ladies and seldom by males around an image. This is a crude form of Rásaḍá), Fera (in Southern Maratha country a rude form of Rásaḍá), Fugaḍi (two females support each other by crossed hands, and revolve with a tremendous speed), etc. are miserably crude and rustic. The professional (of course not tom-tom Nách) or artistic dancing is good, though objectionably surrounded.

Artistic dancing has less technicalities than the drumming. It is worked out with the soles and the big toes of the feet, the right foot performs the major part of it, and "parands" are resorted to as a means to an artistic performance. The ordinary technicalities are few, and they are these:—Tá, Tak, Tad, Thai Tho, Thun, etc.

An artistic way of dancing has not only to look to Tálas (time), but it has to adorn the whole body in regulation with the metres of the feet in combination with different emotions by the features, attitudes, postures, and by gestures. The flourishing of the hands is a necessary condition of the body showing emotions in their full strength. To understand the meaning of flourishing the hands in dancing, as a necessray condition, cannot be completely comprehended by simply reminding ourselves that the acrobatic feats are facilitated by flourishing the hands or the poles to gravitate the body. We, therefore, deviate a little from our immediate subject to study the actions of the arms in walking.

If we place our arms close to our sides, and keep them there while walking with some rapidity, we will unavoidably fall into a backward and forward motion of the shoulders of a wriggling (ungraceful) character. After persevering in this for a space, until we find, as we must, that the action is not only ungraceful but fatiguing, let us suddenly allow our arms to swing as usual. The wriggling of the shoulders will cease, the body will be found to move equably forward, and comparative ease will be felt. On analysing this fact, we may perceive that the backward motion of each arm is simultaneous with the forward motion of the corresponding leg, and, if we will attend to our muscular sensations we will find that this backward swing of the arm is a counterbalance to the forward swing of the leg; and that it is easier to produce that counterbalance by moving the arms than by contorting the body, as we otherwise must do.

The action in the arms in walking being thus understood, it will be clear that the graceful employment of the hands in dancing, is simply an advancement of the same thing.

An artistic dancer is one not only having so acute a muscular sense as at once to feel in what direction the flourishing of the hands should be moved to most readily counterbalance any motion of the body or leg, but having an artistic sense to gracefully adjust them in such a way as to add to the general effect of different postures, of attitudes, and of movements. Those who fail to adjust the hands in an artistic way, give to the audience, of course not an unthoughtful one, the impression that their hands are a trouble to them; they are held stiffly in a meaningless attitude, they are checked from swinging in the directions in which they would naturally swing, ; or they are so moved, that instead of helping to maintain the gracefulness (the principal aim in a dance) they endanger it. A good dancer, on the contrary, makes us feel that, so far from the hands being in the way, they are of great use. Each motion of them, while it seems naturally to result from a previous motion of the body, is turned to some advantage. We perceive that it facilitates instead of hindering the general action of the body or the gracefulness of dancing. As in walking nobody praises a walk that is irregular and jerking, and as nobody sees any gracefulness or beauty in the waddling of a fat man or the trembling step of an invalid; so in dancing nobody admires the dancing that is speedy, perfectly *unrhythmical*, and accompanied by violent swings of the hands.

The reference to walking and dancing suggests that graceful motion, as is said by Spencer, might be defined as motion in curved lines, certainly zig-zag movements are excluded from the suggestion. He says : "The sudden stoppages and irregularities which angular movements imply, are its antithesis : for a leading element of grace is continuity—flowingness"

It will be found that the above saying is merely another aspect of the same truth which we have said before. That as knowledge progresses the mode of impressions and expressions becomes more complex and economical (better adapted, that is, to obtain *the maximum of result with the minimum of energy or force*. This is a fundamental law of nature) in obedience to the law of least resistance and greatest traction or the resultant of the two, which governs motion, physical, psychological and sociological. And in addition to this we say that motion is undulatory or *rhythmical* ; and that motion in curved lines is an economical motion. Instead of giving the metaphysics of motion, we simply refresh our memory by saying that our daily walks, the flights of birds, the paces of graceful dancers, the drills of soldiers, the lines of railways, the foot-paths, the currents of streams, the cadences of orators, poets and singers, etc, are rhythmical or undulatory.

Instead of treating the subject of dancing at length, suffce it to say that the movements or locomotions of the feet, of the hands, of the features, and of the whole body, which we always use in a comparatively irregular form in our daily life, are regulated and advanced as a means to express emotions or centrally-initiated feelings.

If dancing in itself like an art, is debasiug, so are, also, the rhetoric, poetry, and music. Regarded from this point of view, it is unaccountable why the present agitation is directed against dancing wholesale. The same agitation would be better directed, if it were against, or in improving, the Nách and Kairbá of dancing-girls, of Tamáshávalas, of Bhavaiás, and of many others. This sort of fun is not only ludicrous but is an eye-sore.

We cannot pass over without saying a few words on the gesticulations (Háva-Bháva or Arath) or the expressions of emotion by the features and by the movements of the body in artistic dancing. In dancing the expressions of emotion of pain or pleasure, suitable to words (this class of singing always deals more with poetry than with music), are exhibited more vividly by bodily movements than by voice. Certainly, the violent or inordinate emotions of a maniac and the horrible pangs of a sufferer are excluded from this description. Pleasurable feelings are attempted by voice, by flourishing the whole body, by brightening the eyes and by a gentle or graceful smile.

It is hardly necessary to say that while standing, we commonly economize power by throwing the weight chiefly on one leg, which we straighten to make it serve as a column, while we relax the other; and to the same end, we allow the head to lean somewhat on one side. Instead of showing the necessity of using the neck in expressions of emotion, we simply remind ourselves that—that which the photographer does with our sitting, standing, and with adjusting our neck and sight, is better and done more artisically.

In dancing, painful feelings are shown more skilfully than the pleasurable ones, because the muscular action of this kind is much more decided to be imitated. A convulsive start of the whole body (not regardless of Tála or time), is shown by a sudden twinge. A pain is shown by a knitting of the brows, by a biting of the lips, and by the contraction of the features generally. A persistent pain is shown by different attitudes and postures, the body is made to swing to and fro (consistently with the general time of the piece of music), and the hands are clenched. Grief is shown by a wringing of the hands, the shedding of tears and by sighing. And even a pretended action of tearing the hair, cloths and ornaments or adornments, is restored to. A pretended mode of rubbishing the body and of committing suicide by poisons and by every instrument of Asiatic warfare is adopted. Anger is shown in frowns, in distended nostrils, in compressed lips, and in stamping the ground. And even the action of clenching the fingers, of blows of the shoulders, and of elbows and throwing about the clothes and ornaments, is not left in the cold. Discontent is shown by raised eyebrows and by wrinkled forehead. Disgust is shown by a curl of the lips, and offence is shown by a pout. In short, some of the natural expressions of emotion are so artistically performed (there are very few of this description), with due regard to decency and to music, that they give to a patient observer many materials, which a painter or a sculptor may turn to advantage. It is true that the majority of the painful expressions, is a result of the pretended grief, pain, disgust, discontent etc. but it shows in a degree the most unhappy result of poligamy. It is really irreconcilable with the notion of the performer to condemn poligamy, but it is a sentiment of the progressive humanity, and, therefore it predominates in spite of its objectionable surroundings. It is too much to say that monogamy is exclusively human, because there are many kinds of birds and animals, who practise it persistently.

To show the utility of certain gesticulations which we unconsciously practise in our daily life, we draw directly on the most thoughtful writings of Spencer, who is in one with the illustrious Darwin. Spencer says: "How truly language must be regarded as a hindrance to thought, though the necessary instrument of it, we shall clearly perceive on remembering the comparative force with which simple ideas are communicated by signs. To say 'Leave the room,' is less expressive than to point to the door. Placing a finger on the lips is more forcible than whispering 'Do not speak.' A beck of the hand is better than 'come here.' No phrase can convey the idea of surprise so vividly as opening the eyes and raising the eyebrows. A shrug of the shoulders would lose much by translation into words."

To add to the above subject we say "A nodding of the neck with a slight *ye* or *hn* or *hun*" is more expressive than any words of affirmation and approval. "A slight shaking of the neck with a slight *n* or *an* or *un* or *hn*" is more impressive than any words of negation and disapproval. "A slight wrinkle of the nose and of the forehead and a little raising of the cheeks and closing of the eyes with a slight *ish* or *hish* (or something expelling out)" is stronger than any amount of words of disgust and disapprobation. In short, there are numerous but impressive expressions of simple feelings which no form of orthography and of articulate language attempts to imitate. They are too short and inaudible to be covered by music. That branch of grammar, which is called interjection, and which condenses entire sentences into syllables, is too incomplete to give them due justice.

Darwin says that "from the excitement of pleasure the circulation becomes more rapid, the eyes are bright, and the colour of the face rises; and that the brain being stimulated by the increased flow of blood, reacts on the mental power. A man in this state holds his body erect, his head upright, and his eyes open; and that there is no drooping of the features, and no contraction of the eyebrows. To unwrinkle means to be cheerful or merry; and that the whole expression of a man in good spirit is exactly the opposite of that of suffering from sorrow."

C. Bell says: "In all the exhilarating emotions the eyebrows, eyelids, the nostrils, and the angles of the mouth are raised. In the depressing passions it is the reverse. Under the influence of the latter the brow is heavy, the eyelids, cheeks, mouth, and the whole body droop, the eyes are dull, the countenance pallid, and the respiration slow. In joy the face expands, in grief it lengthens."

The subject of dancing and gesticulations cannot be treated at length for want of space. But we can safely pronounce that, that which expresses feelings by bodily actions and movements to which the human flesh is heir, is the manifestation of the waves of nervous influence, which (waves) are the correlative of feelings, presentative, representative and re-representative.

Instead of treating the law of *reflex action* again, let us point out that from that pursuing of the mouth indicative of slight displeasure of a *Savant* in avoiding a false deduction upto the roaring of anger of a savage, and from that mechanism of the muscle (commonly-called) in weaping of a sufferer, —and from that contraction of the zigomatic muscles in a smile of a civilized upto the paroxysm of laughter of a rude man, and from that mechanism of the vocal cords in a whisper of a scandal-monger upto the most complex song of a singer—we find that mental excitement exhibits itself in bodily activity.

Spencer says:—"Before proceeding to the synthetic interpretation, it may be well to remark that even in our ordinary experience, the impossibility of dissociating the psychical states classed as intellectual from those seemingly most unlike psychical states classed as emotional, may be discerned. While we continue to compare such extreme forms of the two as an inference and a fit of anger, we may fancy that they are entirely distinct. But if we examine intermediate modes of consciousness, we shall quickly find some which are both cognitive and emotive.."

In closing this chapter we trust that the broad outlines of Indian music which are given in this and the proceeding chapters, cannot be said to have been accidental and to have been progressed when the said music was in its infancy, neither they can be said to have been borrowed by the ancient Hindus from their contemporary nations. Unhappily that part of Indian music, which is more interesting and instructive from a scientific point of view, has been entirely neglected by ourselves and by our predecessors. We give no theory, but confine our sphere and investigation to the narrower limits of calculating Svaras (notes). Tálas (time), Nritya (dancing) and Háva'-bháva (gesticulation), and thus degrade our music from its higher aspirations to lower pleasures. However, we believe that the evidence, which has been brought forward in our discussion, though of a small magnitude, is sufficient to warrant the leading proposition that Indian music was of higher development than it is generally voted to be and has been dying out for want of support.

Our task will be complete if we now turn our attention to the present state of Indian music.

VI

THE PRESENT STATE OF INDIAN MUSIC

It is neither with a pessimistic notion nor with a sarcastic object we remark that the striking defect of our present singers, is that very few of them are properly trained. This defective training is due, partly to the proverbial unwillingness of Indian musicians to part with their skill unreservedly, and partly to the want of ambition on the part of learners because of the lack of encouragement by the public. No sooner is a voice of some sweetness discovered than it is forced into a hurried drill for a time, the possessor of it is taught to sing a few Chijas (poetry set to music), and is straight way thrust before the public with as much trumpeting as his circumstances can admit of. The singer, after spluttering for a time, gradually subsides into a dead level of mediocrity ; or supposing him to be possessed of taste and perseverance, continues practising, and learns to sing by the time he has lost the major portion of the sweetness of his voice. In good many instances, the possession of a sweet voice is regarded by the owner as amply sufficient for his purpose, and he discards any attempt to acquire an artistic management of it. It is really puzzling that there are many vocalists who did not think it worth their while, to consult a sweetness of the voice as the necessary instrument to singing. There are now, and will no doubt always remain, a few not able exceptions to the above rule; but with the generality of singers there is not the remotest realization of concordance and no endeavour is made to hide defects by a careful and well-considered practice. It is enough that mere accident has given them a sweet voice, and henceforth let indiscriminate praise and patronage do their worst. Smooth and easy singing and graceful and finished phrasing go for nothing, and in their place an amount of shouting, shrieking, violent gesticulations, and comic grimaces are performed. Natural means are always preferable, but the necessary cultivation is of great utility. It is rigorously true, as is said by J. S. Mill and others, that natural is as artificial as artificial is natural, because art has no means independent of Nature. Art is a part and parcel of Nature. The words nature, art, and science, when properly interpreted into thought, are heriditarily transmitted, accumulated and organized experiences of the continuous adjustment of subjective to objective relations which constitute life.

Other false methods of splitting the ear of the groundlings, have also come into vogue, namely, the introduction of high notes screamed out to the fullest extent of the singer's lungs and the practice of Tána (variation or swift jumping) has reached such a tremendous speed, that it can hardly be known by the performer himself, or followed by an artistic ear. Such a tremendous velocity is evidently inadmissible for the want of consonance in Svaras (notes) and in Rágas. It is ridiculous to presume that with such an undue haste of producing the notes, we can maintain a complete preservation of the Svaras (notes), of the principle of ascent and descent, of the Murchhanás and of the distinction of the Rágas. The practical ear is so much accustomed to the principles of Sura (concordance), of Komal-Tivra (half or sharp notes), of Arohan (ascent), of Avarohan (descent), of Mínḍ (connection of notes by tension), of Ghasit (connection of notes by shortening the length of a sonorous body), of Ta'na (variation or jumping), of Murchhana' ($\frac{1}{4}$th part of a tone), of Murki (an advanced form of the trill), of Kamp (shaking or *vibrato* tones), and of Ta'la (time or sequnce) that a slight breach in them is made out, and the performance is regarded not only as inartistic, but most unmusical.

In addition to the aforesaid defects of high notes

and speedy Ta'nas, there is one, which is very intolerable, namely, the introduction of the most complicated, slowest, and of fastest Ta'las. What earthly advantage could there be to the singers who pay more of their attention to the intricate branches of Ta'la, than to the Svaras ?

The Ta'las if normally kept, add to the charm of sound, but if handled most technically they are more puzzling than charming. However, such screaming-notes, speedy Ta nas and chronometric Ta'las are supposed to be the highest aim of the vocal art.

Notes that are too high, are shrill and lose entirely that sweet quality which constitutes the principal characteristic of musical notes. It is strictly true that the aesthetic principles to which the art of music successively confirms, have no absolute value. But it may be said with certainty that no single innovation will ever be accepted, which is clearly in conflict with the broad principles of music, which are reduced by Western philosophers and scientists to one single principle, viz. that musical notes must satisfy the laws of *harmony* and this is the more perfect, the more the notes of *a chord reinforce the fundamental note.*

Sound of fine *timbre* and harmonies of sound have in common the character, that they result from vibrations so related as to cause in the auditory apparatus the least conflict of action and the greatest amount of co-operation, thus producing the largest total of normal excitement in the nerve elements affected.

The high notes, swift Tánas and puzzling Tálas of claptrap are wholly undeserving the attention and support they receive; yet some of the highly praised singers do bring in these sensational means to pander to the liking of the un-deserving and shallow portion of their hearers. Stooping to such an unworthy device to obtain applause and patronage from the unthoughtful audience, which, unhappily, too often form the modern patrons of music, should be repudiated and shaken off by the singers who are capable of better things, and whose artistic conscience must cry shame at such slidings and presumptuous fallacies. Moreover, those on the topmost round of the ladder, should set a noble example to their brethern below. These abnormally high notes and undue liberties in music are always more or less disagreeable to the ear. It may justly be observed that there should be no violation of nearly the only rule in singing, which admits of no excuse—that two unsympathetic (like Vivadi) sounds must not be sounded successively or instantaneously. Such sounds never make a complete fusion, and hence are totally incompatible with music which is a pleasure-giving art.

In order that a chord, produced by three or more notes, may be consonant, it is necessary that the different notes that compose it bear, in respect of the number per second of the vibrations, simple ratios, not only to the fundamental note, but also to each other. It is rigorously true that music, if confined only to consonant chords, and it if does not adopt dissonant chords, would by extremely poor (monotonous).

P. Blaserna says: "Strictly speaking, much greater satisfaction is felt when a dissonant chord is resolved into a consonant chord than when nothing but consonant chord has been heard. It is the force of contrast which produces these sensations in us, just as we doubly appreciate a calm after a storm."

"There can be no absolute rule for the admission of dissonance, and for determining the limit up to which it may be used. All this depends on the degree of musical culture and on habit. Discords which now are perfectly permissible would have appeared monstrosities in the time of Palestrina"

It is necessary to remind the reader that the aforesaid description in no way affects the notes or determinate intervals of a musical scale, but it relates to a composition of those notes or intervals.

Again, how seldom singers are met with who can sing the ancient and old composers' florid music with clearness and flexibility ? And how few, even in the simplest passages of Kirtan (something like *oratorio*), are capable of singing with sufficient religious pathos and fervency, to reach the hearts of their hearers, and thus create in them those agreeable and pleasurable sensations (peripherally-initiated feelings) and emotions (centrally-initiated feelings), which are the most coveted and even called *Nirva'na* (total absorption or eternal happiness), the principal ambition and end of all religious beliefs. This want of skill to produce certain notes in a given time, is sadly observable in our day, and yet instances have been known of the astounding effect and influence, which some of the great singers of past ages had had over their hearers.

It is said of Tansen that when he sang before Haridás, the latter after hearing him with admiration told him :—"Whilst singing you neither stood, nor moved like a human being. This is supernatural, because you have concentreted the whole spirit of your body and mind into the voice. But I tell you these gigantic Gamaks (not jumping), Tánas, Paltás (a kind of variation), Bolatáns (variation of the poetical words in sound and in Tàla. In ordinary singing they do away with the words in Tàna and never-ending notes are only astonishing. Now it is time that you should think of pleasing your audience. You are too young to know your gift, and if you wish to reach the innermost heart, you must take a plainer and a simpler road." These few but most thoughtful words taught the singer a lesson which he never unlearnt, and thenceforth he studied to be effective and pathetic as well as grand and powerful. It is pitiful that many of our much-made-of singers could not receive a similar hint and profit by it.

It was observed more than once that when the late Haddu Khan of Gwallior used to sing to his satisfaction, his band (accompaniment) which consisted of two Tànapurás or Tamburás (four-stringed lyre), two Sárengis (fiddles), two boys or assistants (his sons) and a drummer, left off playing, and, when called attention, confessed that they were so much overpowered with admiration as to be unable to accompany him. No such effects are produced in our day, perhaps, we are getting more artistic than touching !

Haddukhán had held an undisputed sway over his contemporary Khya'l-singers and was credited with having preserved some of the cadences and Khya'ls of Ta'nsen and his successors, though he (Haddukhán) belonged to another family of the great singers of the 19th century. The cadences of Ta'nsen and of many others of the by-gone generations, were transmitted by generation to generation as a patrimony or heritage to the trustworthy and deserving relatives. This mode of confining the transmission and diffusion of music within the limited families and of dealing with it as an article of monopoly, had and has been so strict that it had and has been very difficult, though not impossible, for other families and amateurs to compete on terms of equality. This check has told very heavily on the circulation of Indian music and not only has it stopped further progress of the labour and thought of the by-gone generations, but has injured the art most vitally.

In connection, with the last prodigies of the Hindustani music we cannot pass over without enumerating, out of many, the names of the following artists :—

Vajirkha'n—Dhama'r-singer. Hasukha'n, Haddukha'n and Ta'nraskha'n—Khya'l-singers. Alija'n, Tasduk-Husen and Devaji—Ṭappa' and Tirvaṭ-Tara na -singers. Ba'bu Jotsingji, Kudousing, Joravarsing and Nasarkhán—drummers, Ghula'mali—Swarod-player. Va'rasalikhán—Bina'-player. Sa'dakalikha n—Raba'b-player. Ba'ha'dersenkha'nsa'heb—Raba b and Sursinga'r-player. And the last but not the least the late Gosva'mi Maha ra ja Shri Jivanla'lji (an amateur Sata'r and Bina'-player. The Ma'ha'ra'ja' was an artist in Joḍa in Bilambpada and in Madhya).

The aforesaid artists and a few others were the real artists in our time and whoever heard them and knew their real worth, was never left untouched and unmoved. These artists are not only dead and buried or burnt, but along with them many Ra'gas, cadences, songs, tunes and Parands of the Aryan design and Mahomedan improvement are irretrievably lost, never to reappear in their true form and force.

Language, intellectual or emotional, like organic beings, when once extinct, never reappears. The same language, as has been said by Western philosophers, never has two birthplaces. Distinct languages may be crossed or blended together, but the dominant (not, invariably superior in every respect) languages spread widely and lead to the gradual extinction of other languages.

The Rágas, which are composed by Hardás, (Tánsen's last Usta'd or teacher) Ra mda's, Surda's, Ta'nsen, Bila'skha'n and others, and called after their names, indicate a remarkable degree of the power of composition. The Ra'gas composed by these artists, are not new, but consisted of more than one old Ra'ga melodiously combined. There has been a general belief among the Indian musicians that however new and accomplished a composition of the notes may be, it can be classed under the names of the old Ra'gas, singly or combined.

Oh, but where are our Ta'nsens, Ba'ha'darsenkhánsáhebs and Máhárájás Shri Jivanláljis now? Alas, neither the pathos nor the Joḍas exist. It is true that occasionally some of the imitative pieces of the great vocalists and instrumentalists, are heard, but nothing unusual occurs except a fair execution of a few Rágas and Tánas.

Many vocalists get a name solely for the so called *musical literature* and *Ta'la-Prasta r* (extension), others are liked for Rágas and Tánas, others are praised for Minḍ or Ghasiṭ, others are valued for Murki and Giṭakaḍi, and others are patronized *for vigour and vocal fire-works*. But is there ever heard a mastery of beautiful style combined with a sweet and forcible voice, skill in the management of it, purity of intonations, clearness of phraseology and above all, a capability to entrance the feelings of the hearers, the only object and aim of the evolution of music ?

It is regretable to say that the recitative singing in Nátak (drama), is abnormally degenerated and hybridized. It is true that there are certain mixed airs of the so-called Indian and European music, but they cannot be classed as musical and are also very remote from any kind of perfection. This branch of music seems to be quite misunderstood because of there being no heart, no earnestness and no intelligence thrown into a true state of the legitimate singing. The deplorable fault in Nátak-singing, will not be magnified if it be said that it is the rule and not an exception, that we find but very few actors who can in singing, adjust their voices to the musical instruments and thus save the audience from the discordant and incoherent clatter which counts for singing. Such actors are anything but musical and artistic in expressing the genuine expression of Emotions. And yet such performers are allowed to act in singing and are patronized to become not only troublesome to a degree to the audience appreciating music and emotions, but to spread their so-called airs like a wild-fire throughout their patrons. It is simply ridiculous to see a parade of lads, in female costume, exhibiting fortuitous female feelings and charms.

Again, these interlopers in music think that by reciting their poems aloud or *falsetto* and by a lower or a higher tone at times or alternately, they execute the artistic modulations of voice. Many actors sing as if they have been taught to do certain things without understanding the motive for so doing. Any intelligent critic has only to attend a Nátak (Drama) to see the above facts fully demonstrated. Will the newly-started and much made of Gáyan Samájas (musical congresses of clubs) and schools of music at different quarters, tend to mitigate and alliviate the evil by assuring such actors that what they perform as singing, is no more than a sort of musical declamation of an ordinary type? The answer must, it is feared at the present at all events, remain in abeyance. If the Samájas and schools are unable to improve the Nátak-music, which is the more valued and appreciated, how are they to be credited to regenerate the music which is unalloyed by poetry and stage scenery?

The less we say, the better of our modern poets who unnecessarily mar their, otherwise good, poetries by encumbering them with their big-named Rágas and Tálas.

We know all vocal sounds, when considered by themselves, are musical sounds caused by the vibrations of the vocal cords. Vowels are, as their name implies, the only real vocal sounds; it is only in a vowel that a note can be said or sung. Our speech however is made up not only of vowels, but also of consonants, *i.e.*, of sounds which are produced not by the vibrations of the vocal cords, but by the expiratory blast being in various ways interfered or otherwise modified in its course through the throat and mouth. It is true that distinction between the vowels and consonants is, however, not an absolute one, as the characters of the several vowels depend on the form of the mouth and in the production of some consonants vibrations of the vocal cords do form a necessary though adjutant factor. Whenever we hear a note sounded by the larynx, we are able to recognize in its features one or other of the "vowels" as being uttered. Vowel sounds are in fact only extreme cases of quality, extreme prominence of certain overtones brought about by the shape assumed by the buccal and pharyngeal passages and orifices, as the vibrations pass through them. Each vowel has its approximate and causative disposition of these parts. Each of the "vowel" forms of the mouth possesses a note of its own, one towards which it acts as a resonance chamber.

Max Muller says: "The vowels are produced by the form of the vibrating air. They vary like the *timbre* of different instruments, and we in reality change the instrument on which we speak when we modify the buccal tubes in order to pronounce a, e, i, o and u.

G. P. Field says: "Vowel sounds are rich in overtones and can therefore be heard at a much longer distance. Hence whispering, in which, as the vowel sounds are abated, the consonants are relatively strengthened."

Woolf shows: "The broad A is heard further than any other vowel; and also that, H without an added vowel, is the weakest of all the consonants."

As one of the great triumphs of the present science of Europe, Helmholtz has actually demonstrated the relative pitches and *timbres* of the vowels and has succeeded in making the fundamental pipe *speak* the different vowels in a clearly pronounced manner.

For the high notes singers prefer the "e" and "i", and find it impossible to pronounce "a" and "u" on the highest.

Do our poets know that there are many difficulties in their way to render their poems to the big-named Rágas and Tálas.

Strictly speaking, the laws of music, which are being accumulated and systematized by Western philosophers and scientists and which we have been using throughout our discussion, were certainly not known to our genius-poets and musicians of olden times, who have left an imperishable mark in their respective works. They were guided in their works by feelings, fancy and artistic inspirations.

As the most profound knowledge of Grammar, Syntax and Prosody is not sufficient to make even a mediocre *poet,* so no complex study of the laws of harmony and instrumentation would be sufficient to create a *musician.* Science is directive and art is executive ; the former systematizes, while the latter accumulates.

Singing, when developed to its higher stage of perfection, does away with words as its adjuncts, and produces not only the same influence but better effect.

To return to the thread of our immediate subject, we remark that another cause of deterioration in singing of our day is the strength of Sáth (band or accompaniment) which is the principal hindrance. It is perfectly useless for a best singer in the world to attempt to make himself heard through a number of voices, strings, pipes, bells and parchments played. No human lungs could do such a feat with ease and grace. And yet the experiment of many instruments as accompaniments, is continuously being tried. Most singers think, as if it were a necessity, highly of their band which appears to claim their attention and in good many instances they appear to study nothing else.

With the majority of singers we find 2 boys or assistants, 2 big Tánpurás or Tamborás, 2 big fiddles with as many strings and holes as the instrument can bear and a noisy Pakhávaj or Tablábáyá. In some performances the above list is greatly swelled as a means to melodies by the incoherent and unsympathetic instruments. It should be borne in mind that the audience like to hear the vocalists as well as the instrumentalists. Singers, in making their headway against so many odds and so much power brought literally to play upon them, are seen opening their mouths and we are led to fancy that they are singing ; but, honestly speaking, nothing comes out of their mouths, except the pantomimic action, contortion of the features and above all the most funny and comic expressions of the different phases of anthropomorphous animals, the band efiectually drowning whatever vocal effect might be intended.

Nothing is more pleasurable, elevating and ennobling than to listen to melodies and harmonies produced by trained and sweet voices; and nothing is gained by overpowering them, when it can so easily be avoided.

Singers ought to contrive to keep their band in playing with as little din and noise as possible and to enhance the pleasure of their audience and thus be appreciated. It is necessary for an artistic performance to have an accompaniment of a few instruments as a support and addition to the voice, but it is also very desirable that the instrumentalists should rest satisfied with their opportunity for displaying their skill without attempting to ruin the voice of their co-operator.

It is self-evident that the organ of voice is a musical instrument by the aid of which we communicate our emotional and intellectual feelings and thoughts in their most intimate and delicate shade an instrument so flexible and complete that the most perfect artificial contrivance cannot imitate it in the diversity of shades and qualities, which enable the human voice to express the most varied sentiments and passions.

Spencer says :—"It is generally agreed that the tones of the human voice are more pleasing (because they are very rich in harmonics) than any others. Grant that music takes its rise from the modulations of the human voice under emotion, and it becomes a natural consequence that the tones o that voice should appeal to our feelings more than others; and so should be considered more beautiful than any others."

The most that can be said of the instrumental music, is that it is supplementary. In an advanced stage of musical culture the instrumental music is specialized, and has its own charms.

It will create a capital effect if some of our airs and tunes of artistic value, which are peculiarly adapted to be played by a number of instruments at a time, are widened, extended and reduced to the European *notation,* and are heard through their *bands*. The so-called Native airs, which are played by the bands, and which are selected for the musical boxes, are too unmusical to charm the culvitated ear. Some of the Native princes, no doubt, have their bands taught to play Native airs, and the impression is pleasant, but the airs selected are inartistic. If any enterprising artist of high culture and test were to devote himself to compose new airs and tunes of certain simple and compound Ra′gas and of certain Dhuns with due regard to Tála, and get them performed by the European band, the result cannot be otherwise than charming. As a matter of fact, all the technicalities of Indian classic music, cannot be done adequate justice to by the European instruments as they stand now. We must, however, frankly admit and admire that the European instruments as a class, are superior to the Indian instruments in every respect, except the individual string-instruments which are specialized to execute Minḍ, Ghasiṭ, Murchhaná and Murki, which are the real artistic peculiarities and the charming influences of Indian music.

Apart from the above consideration, we pronounce that on the whole it is easy to perceive that many of the defects of our modern singing, may be ascribed to the increased dimensions of the Sáth (band) and its difficult and fortuitous ways of playing. In this connection we cannot pass over without strongly condemning the false notion of drummers that their aid is required to test the vocalist's or instrumentalist's steadiness (Laya) in Tála (time) by harassing him with the most abstruse technicalities of drumming, as if he had to attend only to Tálas and not to Svaras (notes). A vocalist is a real prodigy when assisted by instrumentalists, but is a helpless victim in the hands of instrumentalists when assailed in sounds by them and in time by the drummer. These beatings of drums, clapping of hands, clashing of cymbals, playing of instruments, and these bowing and blowing with might and main by the instrumentalists, lead to shouting, shrieking, screaming and to the roughness of style on the part of singers, to say nothing of the loss of the purity of tone and the spoiling of voices. It would have puzzled our by-gone celebrities to have their voices driven through a tremendous force which is not uncommonly employed as an accessary to the charm of voice.

It is true that the civilized nations of the West have advanced their music to such a degree of perfection, according to their standard of taste, that they utilize different melodies and harmonies to be sung or played by different voices or instruments simultaneously and successively, and produce an effect which to our ear, is too complex to know and judge. But it may safely be said that the Europeans as nations, are really civilized, progressive and con-considerably free to shake off the old ways which on examination prove to be of no use, and to take to new ones or the better ones. It is, therefore, to be presumed that the effect produced by singing and playing of so many voices and instruments at a time, might not be unmusical, but might be a necessary consequence of constructive, distributive and collective skill which progress involves. Broadly speaking, the present music of Europe seems to be on the ascending branch of the parabola.

It is absurd to say that every form or school of music is absolutely charming to all humanity, but is relatively so—to those who have imbibed from their infancy and have been taught individually, socially, and above all hereditarily. Heriditary transmission applies to psysical as well as phychical peculiarities.

Hence the difference even in the Christan nations of accents and music.

Generally speaking, the Italian music is called simple, intelligible, and melodious ; while the German music is studied, obsure and transcendental. In short, every nation has its special marks in national music.

Doctor Saman, in some interesting remarks on the subject of music, doubts "whether even amongst the nations of Western Europe, intimately connected as they are by close and frequent intercourse, the music of the one is interpreted in the same sense by the others."

In returning to the subject in hand, we say that on enquiries it is found that even Europeans, with all knowledge and notation, are, at times, helpless to reduce to writing the most touching and charming cadences of their great singers. Every art has its own secrets which are taught by personal tuition and apprenticeship. This difficulty stands in the way, as we have said more than once, of many musicians whose performance does not go, as a rule, beyond tom-tom music, and confounds with music proper. Tom-tom music is as separate from the Indian classic music as vulgar language is from Sanskrit.

In connection with the overstraining of voice of which we have said before, the subject of Kharaja or Anuda'tt (grave or bass sound), perhaps, deserves a little attention. That the Kharaja has gradually been lowered to a pitch, which to singers is almost beyond endurance, is an unmistakeable fact ; and it is within the bounds of possibility that further lowering may yet be made. Lowering of voice to the pitch, when its natural harmonics are hardly appreciable to the ear, is not a vocal charm ; but it is a kind of voice considerably shorn, though skilful and difficult, of the harmonics which alone adorn the voice as an indispensable medium to express our thoughts and feelings in their most complex shades. It is true that the tones, in which feelings express themselves, are not always high, but are also deep in comparison with the register or Svaritt.

The tendency to produce a tone of *a very low* pitch, is an established and well-understood sign of anger eventually being used consciously as a threat. The low pitch is indicative of disagreeable feelings such as growling, grumbling, indignation, etc. It is true that disagreeable feelings are also shown in screams and shouts.

When our by-gone artists composed Chijas (poetry set to music in Rágas and Jilhás) they knew that they (Chijas) were within the reach of most voices, and could be delivered without violent efforts ; but transpose them either to a higher or a. lower pitch and see how mighty is the differnce. The result in most cases is neither pleasant to the hearer, nor graceful to the performer, but very often greatly tends to bring splendid natural means to premature decay. Whom are we to blame for such intolerable transpositions of high and low pitches ? The former fault must, we think, be laid at the door of instrumentalists. It is a well-known fact that the higher the pitch, the greater the brilliancy of tone produced on most instruments. The latter fault lies with the singers who in the heat of competing with the instrumentalists, lower the pitch to such a depth that most instruments are incapable of following the voice. It is, however, to be hoped that further steps in the above directions may be stayed and discouraged. One of the best indications to that effect, is the adoption of European wind-instruments (the only defect in them is that they get out of tune soon) to replac the string-instruments which do not give a long current of sound unless produced by a bow, and that too is not in unity or quality with the voice. It is absolutely necessary that the accompanying instruments, excepting the drum, must not be only in *unision,* but must be in quality or *timbre.*

To secure the above end in the best possible way, is to adopt "voice" as an accompaniment with some wind-instruments as support. The accompanying voice should only support and intensify the performing one when it makes a stand. Such an effect will not only be capital, but most touching and impressive. It is rigorously true that the wind instruments are wanting in Ghasiṭ but the performing voice can do its Ghasiṭ without support after a long practice. The present mode of accompaniments, is an anomaly, because the singer and player do not do the same general thing with their means, which the word Sa th (accompaniment) implies.

The high and low pitches the swift Ta'nas (variation) and difficult Ta'las (time) have enormonsly contributed to ruin many a voice and to spoil music. It is most intolerable that musicians as a class try to test the capability of their andience instead of consciously trying to please them. In attempting to overwhelm their audience (who in retaliation frightens the performer with the big-named Ra'gas and Ta'las) with the abstruse technicalities they miserably overlook the pleasurable effect of their art. This stratagem leads to many difficult branches of music, which are more astonishing or frightful than pleasant. Any attempt to cast off the above defects should, we hope, be supported by true lovers of music.

Before dismissing this side of our discussion, we give below a few popular hints, which, if properly adhered to, will considerably improve the present defects of our singing and playing :—

1st.—There should be a sweetness of voice and instruments, and a complete concordance of all the notes to be touched in a piece of music.

2nd.—There should be a sympathetic correspondence of the voice and its accompaniments, and the drummer should try to keep up his time with as delicate a handling as possible and to keep his instrument in tune.

3rd.—The number of the notes of a Ra'ga should be scrupulously preserved even in Mind or Ghasiṭ, in

Murki, in Tána, or in each and every way of going from a note to a note with due regard to the principle of ascent and descent.

4th.—The Murchhanás should be touched by a Minḍ or Ghasiṭ along with the notes on which they depend and never separately, and there should be no stand made on them.

5th.—There should be moderation in pitch, in Minḍ or Ghasiṭ, in Murki, in Tána and in Tála, and the activities wasted away by bodily actions and movements, should be concentrated on the voice and instruments.

Our final task is to treat the present literature on Indian music.

VII

MODERN AUTHORS AND CRITICS ON INDIAN MUSIC

In concluding our discussion, a question of a somewhat delicate natue, concerning music, now crops up, but as it is of great importance, and the remaining vitality of the half-dead Indian music solely depends upon it, the question should not be fearfully shirked under any amount of odium. Such a meterial question cannot at any cost be evaded in this discussion. It may be asked, are not most of our so-called authors and critics of music answerable and responsible for much of the false taste and gross ignorance so palpably displayed and betrayed by our audience ? It is really uncharitable not to presume and not to admit that there are a few able, experienced, and impartial authors and critics, who are capable of doing their self-imposed duty with admiration and authority ; but it is also a fact that there are many more who cannot, with honesty, be classed in the above category.

In the majority of published works and criticisms on Indian music, it is not difficult to discover numberless instances of the gross laxity of the primary laws of music, as an art or a science ; and the main object appears to be to write with pedantic exaggeration something without any knowledge, practical or theoretical, under the proverbially revered and impunitive cloth of an author with the object of praising or dispraising a particular school (form) of music. According to such writers, everything is good or bad as the case may be ; and it is not an uncommon occurrence to find two accounts directly opposed to each other of the same Rága and Tála, not only in ideal judgment, but in matter-of-fact particulars. It is proverbial that tastes vary and differ, but that is no excuse why certain canons of a particular school of music should be entirely respected or disregarded. A few out of many inconsistencies, above referred to, combined with a certain amount of flippancy, unhappily in nine cases out of every ten, appear to constitute the sum and substance of modern works and criticisms on Indian music.

There is no standard work on Indian music in any of the spoken languages of the present age, no school is regularly constituted, no competent masters to teach music unreservedly, no examinations are held by professors of music, and in fact no knowledge of the art ; but as equivalent of so many conditions which progress presupposes, we have good deal of impudence and conceit, a vast amount of assumptions and presumptions, and these together with much of the ordinary gloss of the present age, seem to make up the sum total of an author or critic as a recognized stock-in-trade. There is firing and throwing together of words and intricate phraseology, culled from old works of music, or from a Sanskrit Kosha (Dictionary), which, on an artistic or scientific examination, mostly turn out to be simply meanningless grandiloquence that ever soiled a paper. And yet such nonsenses are printed and quoted to help to mislead and to misguide our otherwise enlightened and not easily to be deceived public opinion.

Anybody with a commonplace knowledge of the subject, with a literal insight into the technicalities of Suddha (Diatonic), of Komala (Chromatic), of Tar Tivra (sharper), of Ati-Komala (very flat), of Oḍhava (Rága with 5 notes), of Khaḍava (6 notes), of Sampurna (7 notes), of Sankirna (gleaned or compounded), of A′rohan (ascent), A′varohan (descent), of Shrutis (ratio of the Saptak or scale), of Murchhaná ($\frac{1}{4}$th part of a tone), of Gráma (collection, musically meaningless), of Prastára (extension), of Tála (sequence) of Minḍ or Ghrashaṭak (sliding), and a knowledge of the Sanskrit literature, thinks himself amply justified in giving to the public his works and opinions, and would write with all the airs, as if he had all the intricacies of the art or science, as the case may be, at his finger's end. These so called authors and critics have not the least idea of the theory of musical sounds, nor have they the knowledge of how to produce voice musically. They do not know the real distinction between velocity, intensity, pitch and quality of sound. Nor have they a clear comprehension of the construction and capability of musical instruments. They are unable to realize a Ra'ga or possibly a sound correctly when emitted by voice or by instruments, and are utterly ignorant of the science of melody and its later offspring harmony. In short, such writers are perfect strangers to the physical, psychological, and sociological evolution of sound. And yet these so-called authors and critics presume to pass an elaborate judgment, not only on music of the Hindu design and Mahomadan improvement, as well as on the musicians who have devoted their whole life to study their art, but on also the European music which is one of the real wonders of the 19th century. These self-constituted professors and authors fancy that, by reading a little literature on music and by mere attempts at learning it, they are sufficiently qualified to say whatever they like on it.

Practical experience and theoretical perception in every branch of knowledge, are commonly unattainable by an individual to a very great extent, and the want may be allowed for, if it is not exclusive of each other, but there is a fair proportion so as not to be prejudicial to each other. To make oneself a practical artist, it is desirable that he should know the primary laws of the scientific aspect of his art, but at the same time it is not necessary that he should master the most complex scientific details to learn singing and know how to reach the heart with sweet and skilled voice. History and the living instances of Europe amply confirm the above fact.

P. Blaserna says : "I will content myself by saying that in our modern music art has outstripped science with rapid strides, and it is only quite recently that the latter has been able to give complete and rational explanation of what the former has effected by means of delicate æsthetic feeling. Science cannot desire to be substituted for art."

N. Lockyer, in his translation of the "Forces of Nature", says—"If we mean by musical sounds those which an artist thinks right to introduce into his work to add to the desired effect, not only must those sounds be closely connected by bonds, which are determined by the pitch and duration, but they must unite certain particular qualities, the examination of which pertains more to the domain of art than that of seience."

A. Bain says: "But high scientific knowledge manifestly transcends the sphere of Art, just as a highly artistic form transcends the sphers of science. If it were otherwise, we should be great gainers. If what give us knowledge and certainty as regards the world were also of easy comprehension, and the source of light and fascinating amusement, we should be saved from many pains, and take much higher strides of advancement in the happiness and security of life."

Spencer says that among men a vague notion prevails that the scientific knowledge differs in nature from common knowledge. He conclusively shows that there is no absolute line of demarcation between the two, because the same faculties are employed in both cases and their mode of operation is fundamentally the same. Even the common actions of man presuppose facts colligated, inferences drawn, results expected, and general success of these actions proves the data by which they were guided to have been correctly put together. He, after analysing the subject at length, which for want of space we cannot bring out here, says:—"It is a difference not between common knowledge and scientific knowledge, but between the successive phases of science itself, or knowledge itself—whichever we choose to call. In its earlier phases science attains only to certainty of knowledge, in its later phases it further attains to completeness. We begin by discovering a relation: We end by discovering the relation. Our first achievement is to foretell the kind of phenomena which will occur under specific conditions: our last achievement is to foretell not only the kind but the amount. Or, to reduce the proposition to most definite form—undeveloped science is qualitative prevision: developed science is quantitative prevision. . . . And this is the difference which leads us to consider certain orders of knowledge as scientific when contrasted with knowledge in general." . . .

"So close, indeed, is the relationship, that it is impossible to say where science begins and art ends. All the instruments of the natural philosopher are the products of art; the adjusting one of them for use is an art; there is art in making an observation with one of them; it requires art properly to treat the facts ascertained; nay, even the employing established generalizations, to open the way to new generalizations, may be considered as art. In each of these cases previously organized knowledge becomes the implement by which new knowledge is got at: and whether that previously organized knowledge is embodied in a tangible apparatus or in a formula, matters not in so far as its essential relation to the new knowledge is concerned. If as, no one will deny, art is applied knowledge, then such portion of the scientific investigation as consists of applied knowledge is art. So that we may even say that as soon as any prevision in science passes out of its originally passive state, and is employed for reaching other previsions, it passes from theory into practice—becomes science in action—becomes art. And when we thus see how purely conventional is the ordinary distinction, how impossible it is to make any real separation—when we see not only that science and art were originally one; that the arts have perpetually assisted each other; that there has been a constant reciprocation of aid between the sciences and arts, but that the sciences act as arts to each other, and that the established part of each science becomes an art to the growing part—when we recognize the closeness of these associations, we shall the more clearly perceive that as the connexion of the arts with each other has been ever becoming more intimate, as the help given by sciences to arts and by arts to sciences, has been age by age increasing; so the interdependence of the sciences themselves has been ever growing greater, their mutual relations more involved, their *consensus* more active.

In returning to the subject in hand, we remark that the so-called authors and critics are increasing now-a-days at the expense of the artists and the public at large.

It is true that composition and criticism are diametrically opposite operations of the human mind: they ought to go hand in hand, and as far as possible with a common agreement, and be complementary one to the other; but the critic will never be a great composer, nor the composer a true critic.

Clever artists must laugh when they read—if they ever do—the mass of stuff written concerning their art, of which they have made a life-long study; and yet their experience and knowledge do not allow them to presume and pretend to promulgate a practice or theory of sound, and to impose and practise on public credulity. It is amply justifiable and not too much to pronounce that, if the so-called authors and critics are called upon to submit to an examination to adjust or to find out the difference between the four strings but two notes of Tamborá (four-stringed lyre)—the A B C of the Indian musician, we shall find the percentage of success not only microscopic, but their presumptions and pretensions are sure to vanish in the air.

What bitterness must arise in the mind of artists at times when they cogitate over the power that is wielded by these misleaders of the public opinion?

Power used with discretion, is a desideratum, but becomes a nuisance when used recklessly, at random, and now and then for a motive worthy of nothing but misplaced confidence in one's own abilities.

Again, are not works ever and anon written to propound a particular practice of the Rágas and Tálas, which was never in existence? The major portion of the published music contains a substance which, if reproduced as a vocal or instrumental art, would hardly please the cultivated ear for which it has professedly been published and trumpeted. Many of these authors are fabulous, others are superstitious, and others are full with mythology. None of them, even after a great deal of verbosity, can answer the needful treatment of music, as an alluring and ennobling art, and of its grand evolution to rejoice an innumerable species of animals, man included, with complex sensations (peripherally-initiated feelings), and emotions (centrally-initiated feelings), peculiar to each species and special to each race and its sub-divisions, and of its formation to constitute a part of that whole—a whole which is instrumental in increasing the average length and happiness of individual, family, tribal, national, and human life—a whole which is the force (human activities in their individual and social welfare) that governs and promotes civilization as a means to an end.

Whatever ascetic morality may say, pleasures and pains are the incentives and restrictions by which life is prolonged and multiplied. No contemptuous title of pig-philosophy, as is said by Western philosophers, will alter the eternal law, (so long as life exists), that Misery is the high way to death; while happiness is added Life, and the giver of life. Life, individual and social, on a rational plan, is not of an asceticism; but of full enjoyment in the performance of function and the gratification of senses without endangering the equal happiness of other men. It is an established induction of, and deduction from, the hypothesis of Evolution that pains are the correlatives of actions injurious to the organism, while pleasures are the correlatives of actions conducive to its welfare.

A. Bain says :—"It is a fact of great practical importance that fellow-feeling requires us to have a certain regard to our own happiness in the first instance. If our lot contains but a small share of pleasure, or, if by an ascetic culture we are made to set little value on the enjoyment of life, we part with the very basis of sympathy. Thus, while a large amount of self-regard excludes sympathy, self-abnegation and misery extinguish it. There is a certain middle point between the two extremes, where fellow-feeling is most likely to flourish."

J. S. Mill says : - "That men need not be comfortable themselves in order to enter into discomforts of others ; virtue and wretchedness are incompatible."

H. Spencer says :—"Here, as in every case, there can be no altruistic feeling but what arises by sympathetic excitement of a corresponding egoistic feeling ; and hence there can never be a sense of justice to others when there is not a sense of justice to self, at least equally great. . . . Societies, past and present, supply ample evidence of these relations. At the one extreme, we have the familiar truth that the type of nature which readily submits to slavery, is a type of nature equally ready to play the tyrant when occasion serves. At the other extreme, we have the fact well-illustrated in our own society, that along with the increasing tendency to resist aggression, there goes a diminishing tendencv on the part of those in power to aggress." . . .

"The conflict that has hitherto gone on in every society between the predatory life and the industrial life, has necessitated a corresponding conflict between modes of feelings appropriate to the two, and there have similarly been necessitated conflicting standards of right. But now that the pain-inflicting activities are less habitual, and the repression of the sympathies less constant, the altruistic sentiments, which find their satisfaction in conduct that is regardful of others and so conduces to harmonious co-operation, are becoming stronger. The sacredness of life, of liberty, of property, are more and more vividly felt as civilization advances."

Again, none of our so-called and much-made of authors are scientific, however boasting and noisy they may be, to explain and convince that Sound is a transformation or equivalent of Heat or molecular motion, and in itself is a wave of sonorous vibrations caused by the purcussion and friction or by both of solids, liquids and gasses against each other or between themselves. Such authors cannot give us a tangible theory of the phenomenon of sound and prove that it is not universal like gravitation, but is confined to the earth within the limits of atmosphere although in various degrees in torrid, tropical and temporate zones. They also cannot teach us to explain—that sound is conspicuously absent from the antartic, arctic and frigid regions, and is totally absent from a complete vacuum and inter-stellar spaces due to the absence of elastic bodies and tangible media—the necessary condition for the expenditure of heat or manifestation of *Sound* and to explode to pieces the "Nádo-Brahm" notion of the early Hindus.

Do our so-called psychologists know that what we call feelings, sensational, perceptional, and emotional, are the concomitant nervous changes or the waves of nervous influence? Do they also know that by virtue of the general law of nervo-motor action, every feeling has for its primary concomitant a diffused nervous discharge, which excites the muscles at large, including those of the vocal organs, in a degree proportionate to the strength of feeling, and therefore muscular activity increases in amount—be the nature of feeling what it may? Again, do our misnomers comprehend that deep down in the nervo-muscular structures, as they have been evolved by converse between the organism and its environment, are to be found the cause of all the manifestations; and that in the nature of things there have grown up these connexions between internal feelings and external manifestations? It is beyoud the reach of our so-calied psychologists to grasp that a secondary concomitant of feeling in general as it rises in intensity, is an excitement by the diffused discharge, first of the small muscles attached to easily-moved parts, afterwards of morenumerousand large muscles moving heavier parts, and eventually of the whole body.

In short, such self-styled and self-praised philosophic and scientific authors and critics are incapable of comprehending that the production of Sound by animals, is a necessary manifestation of the nervous and muscular force generated and expended by the impressions and expressions which constitute life—as continuous adjustment of internal (subjective) to external (objective) relations—philosophically called *Natural Selection* or *Survival of The Fittest*; and that the intensity of Sound demonstrates the strength of feelings involved; and that the change of Sound is an indicator of the variety of sentiments and passions aroused.

Through the instrumentality of such sham writers and critics many a talented artist has hopelessly been driven out of the patronage which he otherwise richly deserves, and the cause of regenerating Indian music, is not only retrograded and obscured, but the music of Hindu design and Mahomedan improvement of many centuries, is shamelessly forced to die an accelerated death.

That the cultivation of music has no effect on the mind, few will be absurd enough to contend. Every civilized nation (past and present) rationally believes that in its bearing upon human happiness, the emotional language, which musical culture develops and refines, is second to none; and that music has an effect beyond the immediate pleasure it produces, because every class of rational enjoyment does not end with itself, but ministers to bodily and mental well-being. Our nature is such that in fulfilling each desire we in some way facilitate the fulfilment of the rest.

Music in which we discover the synthesis of one of the grandest evolutions of human feeling—is an evolution that in itself forms one of the most brilliant pages in the history of human culture.

The illustrious Darwin, in his "Expression of Emotions" says : "That the chief expressive actions exhibited by man and the lower animals, are now innate or inherited—that is, have not been, learnt by the individual—is admitted by everyone. So little has hearing or imitation to do with several of them that they are from the earliest days and throughout life quite beyond our control, for instance, the relaxation of the certain muscles of the skin in blushing and the increased action of the heart in anger. We may see children, and even these born blind blushing from shame, and the naked sculp of every young infant reddens from passions. If infants scream from pain or frown disapproval, we readily perceive sympathy in others by their expression, our sufferings are thus mitigated and our pleasure increased, and mutual good feeling is thus strengthened. The movements of expression give vividness and enegy to our spoken words. They reveal the thoughts and intentions of others more truly than do words which may be falsified. The first expression of our outward signs of an emotion, intensifies it. On the other hand, the repression, as far as this is possible, of all outward signs softens our emotion. These results follow partly from the intimate relation which exists between almost all the emotions and their outward manifestations ; and partly from the direct influence of exertion on the heart, and consequently on the brain. Even the simulation of an emotion tends to arouse it in our minds. We also know that expression in itself..., is certainly of importance for the welfare of mankind."

Illustrious Herbert Spencer, in his finishing remark on the principles of psychology, philosophically says :—"The æsthetic feelings and sentiments are not, as our words and phrases lead us to suppose, feelings and sentiments that essentially differ in origin and nature from the rest. They are nothing else than particular modes of excitement of the faculties, sensational, perceptional, and emotional—faculties which, otherwise excited, produce those other modes of consciousness constituting our ordinary impressions, ideas, and feelings. The same agencies are in action ; and the only difference is in the attitude of consciousness towards its resulting states."

"Throughout the whole range of sensations, perceptions, and emotions which we do not call as æsthetic, the states of consciousness serve simply as aids and stimuli to guidance and action. They are transitory, or if they persist in consciousness some time, they do not monopolize the attention : that which monopolizes the attention is something ulterior, to the effecting of which they are instrumental. But in the states of mind we class as æsthetic, the opposite attitude is maintained towards the sensations, perceptions, and emotions. They are no longer links in the chain of states which prompt and guide conduct. Instead of being allowed to disappear with merely passing recognition, they are kept in consciousness and dwelt upon : their natures being such that their continued presence in consciousness is agreeable."

"Before this action of the faculties can arise, it is necessary that the needs to be satisfied through the agency of sensational, perceptional, and emotional excitements shall not be urgent. So long as there exist strong cravings arising from bodily wants and unsatisfied lower instincts, consciousness is not allowed to dwell on these states that accompany the actions of the higher faculties : the cravings continually exclude them."

"The activities of this order begin to show themselves only when there is reached an organization so superior, that the energies have not to be wholly expended on the fulfilment of material requirements from hour to hour."

..."When, however, a long discipline of social life decreasingly predatory and increasingly peaceful, has allowed the sympathies and resulting altruistic sentiments to develop, these, too, begin to demand spheres of superfluous activity. Fine art of all kinds takes forms more and more in harmony with these sentiments."

"A final remark worth making is, that the æsthetic activities in general may be expected to play an increasing part in human life as evolution advances. Greater economization of energy, resulting from superiority of organization, will have in the future effects like those it has had in the past. The order of activities to which the æsthetics belong, have been already initiated by this economization, will hereafter be extended by it: the economization being achieved both directly through the improvement of all appliances, mechanical, social, and other. A growing surplus of energy will bring a growing proportion of the æsthetic activities and gratifications, and while the forms of art will be such as yield pleasurable exercise to the simpler faculties, they will in a greater degree than now appeal to the higher emotions."

To a patriotic Indian nothing is more mournful than to see the dying out of Indian music which in its grandeur must have attracted innumerable heads and hearts at times and places.

Oh, why are not our public equally, if not more, thoughtful as they are in matters, political and educational? And why are they so easily led away by the so-called authors and critics on Indian music, in spite of their patriotism which is the most marked trait of modern civilization? And above all, why do not those of the professional and amateur musicians critics and authors, who are capable of better things than those aforesaid, set their feet on the shameful system of bogus writings and criticisms, and thus save and revive the half-dead Indian music from its total annihilation or transformation to a hybrid class—a music that must have in its glory rejoiced many a generation of the ancient and old Indians by its solacing, ennobling, and, above all, charming influence—an influence for which music as a whole has been brought into requisition, not only by the civilized Europeans, Americans, Asiatics and Africans, but by the human race as a whole—a whole composed of the most horrible savage of the forest and the most thoughtful philosopher of the world—the world in which savages transform into families, families into tribes, tribes into communities, communities into nationalities, and nationalities into internationalities, and internationalities in their turn concentrate their collective knowledge or experience into philosophers and philosophers i their turn, after exhausting all possible knowledge in explaining the immutable laws of the inorganic, organic and superorganic evolution and dissolution, stop and conclude :—To *think* is to *condition* ; and conditional limitation is the fundamental law of the possibility of thought. For as the greyhound cannot outstrip his shadow, nor the eagle outsoar the atmosphere in which he floats, and by which alone he may be supported, so the mind cannot transcend that sphere of limitation, within and through which exclusively the possibility of thought is realized. Thought is only of the conditioned, because to think is simply to condition. The *absolute* is conceived merely by a negation of conceivability, and all that we know, is only known as—Won From the Void And Formless Infinite.

FINIS